Graphic Medieval History

CRUSADES

By Gary Jeffrey & Illustrated by Terry Riley

 Crabtree Publishing Company
www.crabtreebooks.com

Crabtree Publishing Company
www.crabtreebooks.com
1-800-387-7650

Publishing in Canada
616 Welland Ave.
St. Catharines, ON
L2M 5V6

Published in the United States
PMB 59051, 350 Fifth Ave.
59th Floor,
New York, NY 10118

Published in **2014 by CRABTREE PUBLISHING COMPANY.**

Printed in Canada/032014/MA20140124

Copyright © 2013 David West Children's Books

Created and produced by:

David West Children's Books

Project development, design, and concept:

David West Children's Books

Author and designer: Gary Jeffrey

Illustrator: Terry Riley

Editor: Kathy Middleton

Proofreader: Adrianna Morganelli

Production coordinator and

 Prepress technician:

 Ken Wright

Print coordinator:

 Margaret Amy Salter

Photo credits:

 p5top, Berthold Werner

Library and Archives Canada Cataloguing in Publication

Jeffrey, Gary, author
    Crusades / Gary Jeffrey ; illustrator: Terry Riley.

(Graphic medieval history)
Includes index.
Issued in print and electronic formats.
ISBN 978-0-7787-0397-6 (bound).--ISBN 978-0-7787-0403-4
(pbk.).--ISBN 978-1-4271-7509-0 (html).--ISBN 978-1-4271-7515-1
(pdf)

    1. Crusades--First, 1096-1099--Juvenile literature. 2.
Hattin, Battle of, Israel, 1187--Juvenile literature. 3. Crusades--
Third, 1189-1192--Juvenile literature. 4. Crusades--First, 1096-
1099--Comic books, strips, etc. 5. Hattin, Battle of, Israel, 1187--
Comic books, strips, etc. 6. Crusades--Third, 1189-1192--Comic
books, strips, etc. 7. Graphic novels. I. Riley, Terry, illustrator
II. Title. III. Series: Jeffrey, Gary. Graphic medieval
history.

D157.J45 2014   j909.07   C2014-900359-5
                                            C2014-900360-9

Library of Congress Cataloging-in-Publication Data

Jeffrey, Gary.
 Crusades / by Gary Jeffrey ; illustrated by Terry Riley.
  pages cm. -- (Graphic medieval history)
 Includes index.
 ISBN 978-0-7787-0397-6 (reinforced library binding : alkaline
paper) -- ISBN 978-0-7787-0403-4 (paperback : alkaline paper) -
- ISBN (invalid) 978-1-4271-7515-1 (electronic html) -- ISBN
978-1-4271-7509-0 (electronic pdf)
 1. Crusades--Juvenile literature. 2. Crusades--Comic books,
strips, etc. 3. Civilization, Medieval--Juvenile literature. 4.
Civilization, Medieval--Comic books, strips, etc. 5. Graphic
novels. I. Riley, Terry, illustrator. II. Title.

 D157.J44 2014
 909.07--dc23

                                        2014002258

Contents

The First Crusade

Even before the start of the Middle Ages, Christians from Europe had traveled to the eastern Mediterranean to worship at the site of Jesus Christ's tomb in Jerusalem. After Muslims conquered the Holy Land in 638 CE, the area still stayed open to pilgrims.

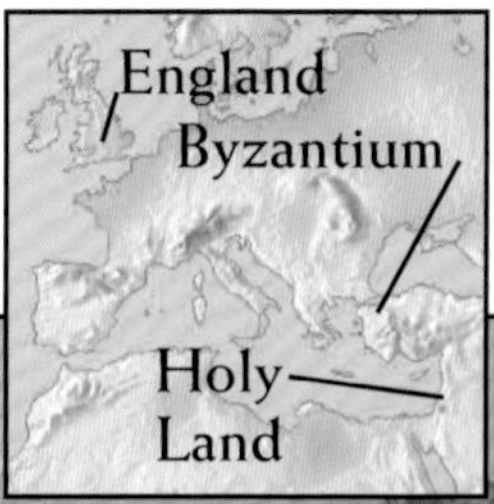
England
Byzantium
Holy Land

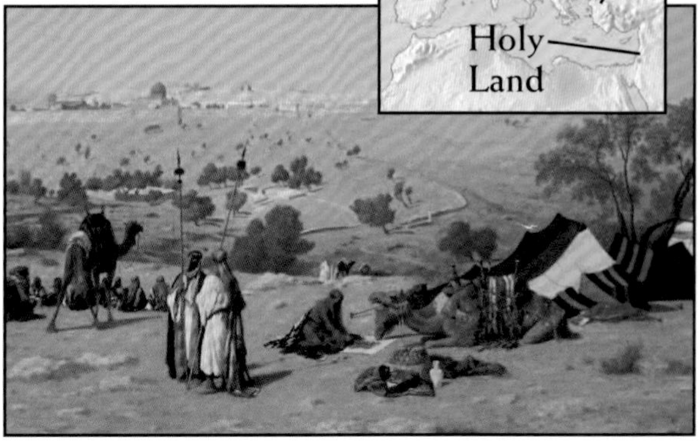

The Eastern Mediterranean (inset) is the birthplace of the religions of Judaism and Christianity. Jerusalem (above) is also where Islam's prophet Muhammad rose up to heaven.

Under Threat

In 1009, the ruler of Egypt, Al-Hakim—a member of the Fatimid dynasty, believed to be descended from the prophet Muhammad—ordered the Holy Sepulcher (Christ's tomb) be destroyed and all Christians persecuted, or treated cruelly or killed for their beliefs. After he died, Al-Hakim's son was persuaded to rebuild the site and reopen it to pilgrims. However, in 1070, Jerusalem and the Holy Land were closed again when the area fell to the Seljuq Turks. Afterward, the Seljuqs also took territory in Byzantium, threatening the eastern Christian empire.

A Call to Arms

Byzantine emperor Alexios I Komnenos asked Pope Urban II, head of the Christian Church, for aid against the Seljuqs. In 1095, Urban called for the Holy Land to be taken back from Muslim control for Christian pilgrimage. With the Pope's promise that the Church would excuse all their sins in return for military service on crusade, many knights "took up the cross" over the next 200 years.

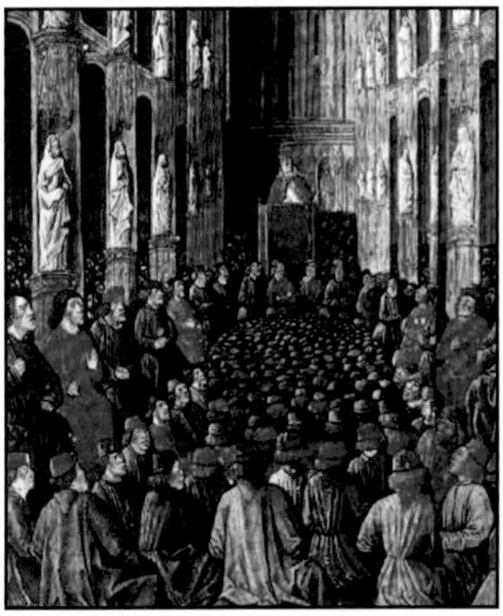

The response to Pope Urban's plea was enormous. Hundreds of knights decided to become "croisée," or crusaders. Croisée is a French word that means "being marked with the cross."

God's Warriors

A group of peasants inspired by a charismatic priest called Peter the Hermit went on their own crusade. Inexperienced in warfare, most of the peasants were slaughtered by the Turks in battle. Meanwhile, Count Raymond of Toulouse, Duke Godfrey of Bouillon, and Italian Bohemond of Taranto, along with other nobles from the western Roman empire led a force into Asia Minor (modern Turkey). They took Armenia, and formed the first crusader state—the County of Edessa.

Antioch fell next after a difficult siege. The crusader leaders squabbled over who would be king. Finally Raymond and Godfrey left for Jerusalem, leaving Bohemond to rule.

While besieged in Antioch, a lance, or spear, was discovered by the crusaders. Their belief that this was a holy relic inspired them to overcome their enemies outside the city.

Eyes on the Prize

They passed by Tripoli, which fell later in 1109. By the time they reached Jerusalem on June 7, 1099, the crusaders were badly in need of water and food. The lucky arrival at Jaffa of ships from Genoa, Italy saved them. With wood from the ships, the knights, who had survived three hard years of campaigning, threw themselves into building siege engines—machines that hurl large rocks—strong enough to conquer the walls of the holy city. The battle for Jerusalem had begun (see page 8).

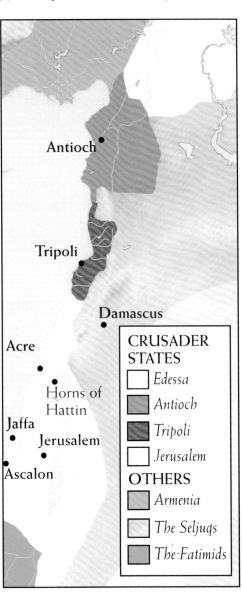

The first crusade to the Holy Land created the crusader states of Edessa, Antioch, Tripoli, and Jerusalem. Surprisingly, at Jerusalem, the crusaders faced the Fatimids who had retaken the city—not the Seljuqs.

(Map labels: Antioch, Tripoli, Damascus, Acre, Horns of Hattin, Jaffa, Jerusalem, Ascalon)

CRUSADER STATES
- Edessa
- Antioch
- Tripoli
- Jerusalem

OTHERS
- Armenia
- The Seljuqs
- The Fatimids

Crusader Kings

To protect pilgrims and help crusaders, military religious orders of "warrior monks" were formed such as the Knights Templar and the Knights Hospitaller. Baldwin II is shown here giving them lodgings.

In 1100, a French nobleman became King Baldwin I of Jerusalem, the jewel in the crown of the crusader states. But success had its price. With their pilgrimage completed and their sins forgiven, thousands of crusaders returned home, leaving the newly Christian territories badly guarded and open to attack.

TROUBLE IN OUTREMER

The Holy Land, called Outremer, or "overseas," by the French, survived under Christian control for over 40 years. But in 1144, Edessa fell to Zengi, the founder of a powerful Seljuq dynasty that ruled parts of Syria. Zengi began a "jihad," or holy war, against the crusader states. In response, Pope Eugene III called for a second crusade, which was led by Louis VII of France and Conrad III of Germany. Their combined force of 8,500 gathered together with 550 Outremer knights near Jerusalem in the city of Acre, where it was decided to give up Edessa and attack Damascus in Syria instead. The siege in 1148 failed.

Christian soldiers were killed by the Islamic warriors they called Saracens. The Saracens called the crusaders Franks.

RISE OF THE AYYUBIDS

The 1170s saw the rise of Saladin, a member of the Ayyubid family (Kurdish soldiers of Zengi). He became a high official of Egypt and then its sultan. Saladin united all the Islamic groups in the Middle East. By 1183, his dynasty controlled Egypt, Syria, and much of North Africa and the Middle East—and posed a great threat to the future of Outremer.

ROAD TO WAR

In 1177, Saladin attempted an invasion of Palestine but was held off by the king of Jerusalem, Baldwin IV, and a force of Knights Templar.

Ruins of the crusader fortress of Kerak in Jordan.

Raynald of Chatillon, a veteran of the crusades, led the resistance.

By 1185 Saladin and Raynald had reached a truce. This was broken in 1186 when Raynald stormed out of his fortress in Kerak and raided Saladin's trade caravans, which were traveling between Egypt and Syria. Saladin-besieged Kerak. Baldwin IV died, and his sister Sybilla succeeded him. Sybilla chose a crusader, Guy of Lusignan, to be her

Richard I being anointed as king.

husband and crowned him king. The inexperienced newcomer wanted to prove he was a strong leader and formed a big crusader army. With this he planned finally to defeat Saladin in battle (see page 20).

THE THIRD CRUSADE

After the battle against Guy of Lusignan, Saladin reconquered all of the Holy Land except for Tyre, Tripoli, and Antioch. A third crusade was called, with English king Richard I and French king Philip II eagerly taking up the cross.

Muslims in Acre were being besieged by Outremers, who were themselves surrounded by Saladin's forces. The arrival of the crusaders broke the stalemate, and Acre surrendered to them on July 12, 1191.

Richard I was an experienced fighter and damaged Saladin's reputation by defeating a large-scale Muslim attack at Arsuf, capturing and holding Jaffa, and occupying Ascalon. Knowing that Saladin's army was disbanding for winter, Richard and his crusaders decided to march on Muslim-held Jerusalem.

King Philip returned to France after three months but left behind 10,000 men to fight on in the crusade.

The Siege of Jerusalem
The First Crusade

JERUSALEM, PALESTINE, JULY 14, 1099. AT DAYBREAK A MASSIVE PIECE OF MARBLE SAILED TOWARD THE CITY WALL EAST OF ST. STEPHEN'S GATE.

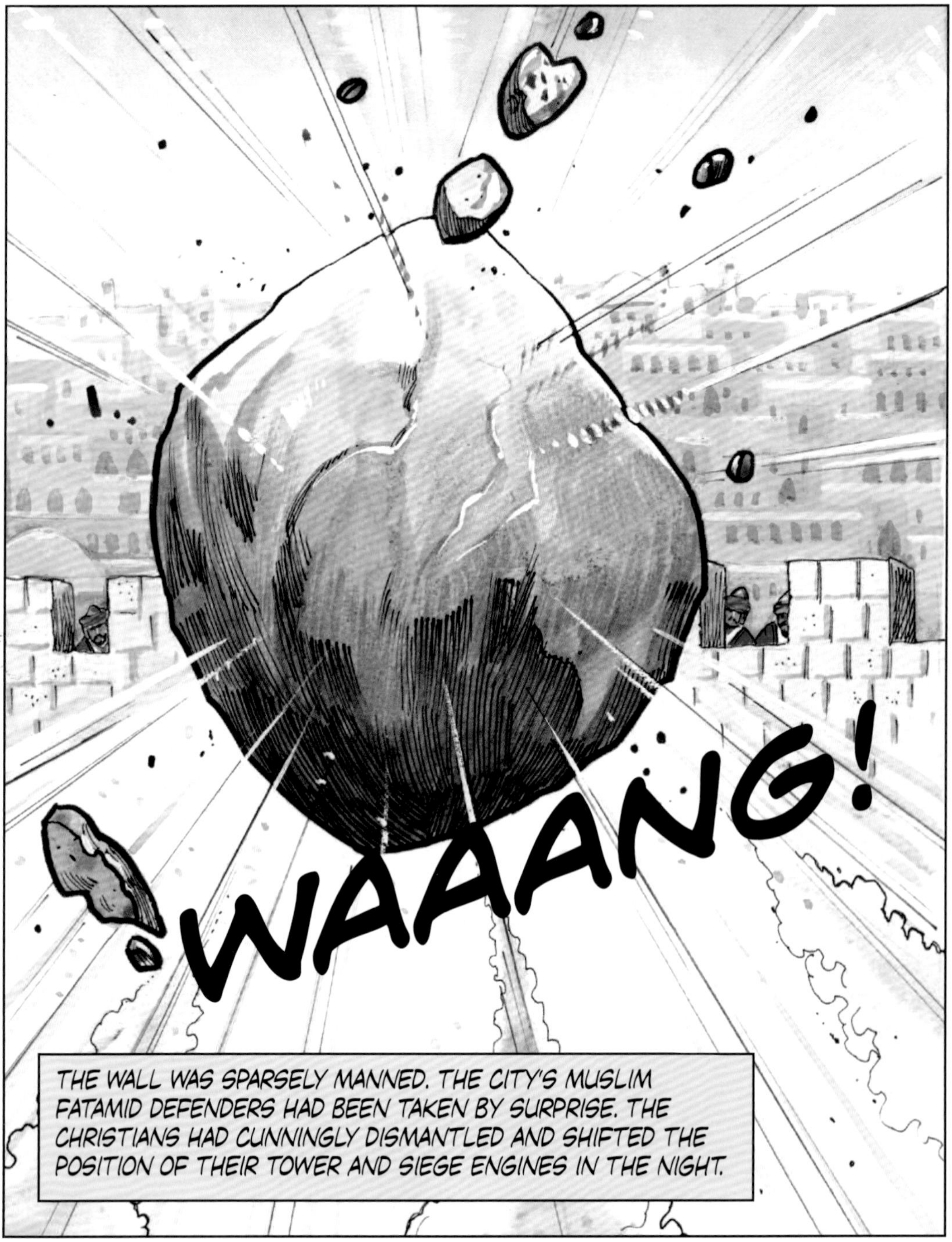
WAAAANG!
THE WALL WAS SPARSELY MANNED. THE CITY'S MUSLIM FATAMID DEFENDERS HAD BEEN TAKEN BY SURPRISE. THE CHRISTIANS HAD CUNNINGLY DISMANTLED AND SHIFTED THE POSITION OF THEIR TOWER AND SIEGE ENGINES IN THE NIGHT.

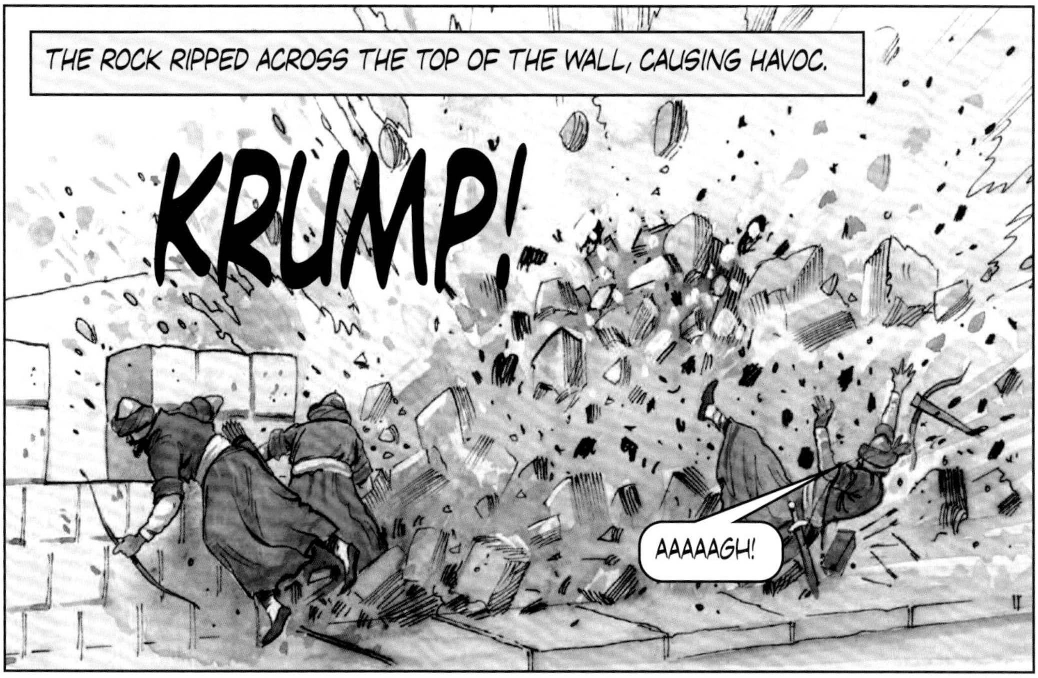
THE ROCK RIPPED ACROSS THE TOP OF THE WALL, CAUSING HAVOC.
KRUMP!
AAAAAGH!

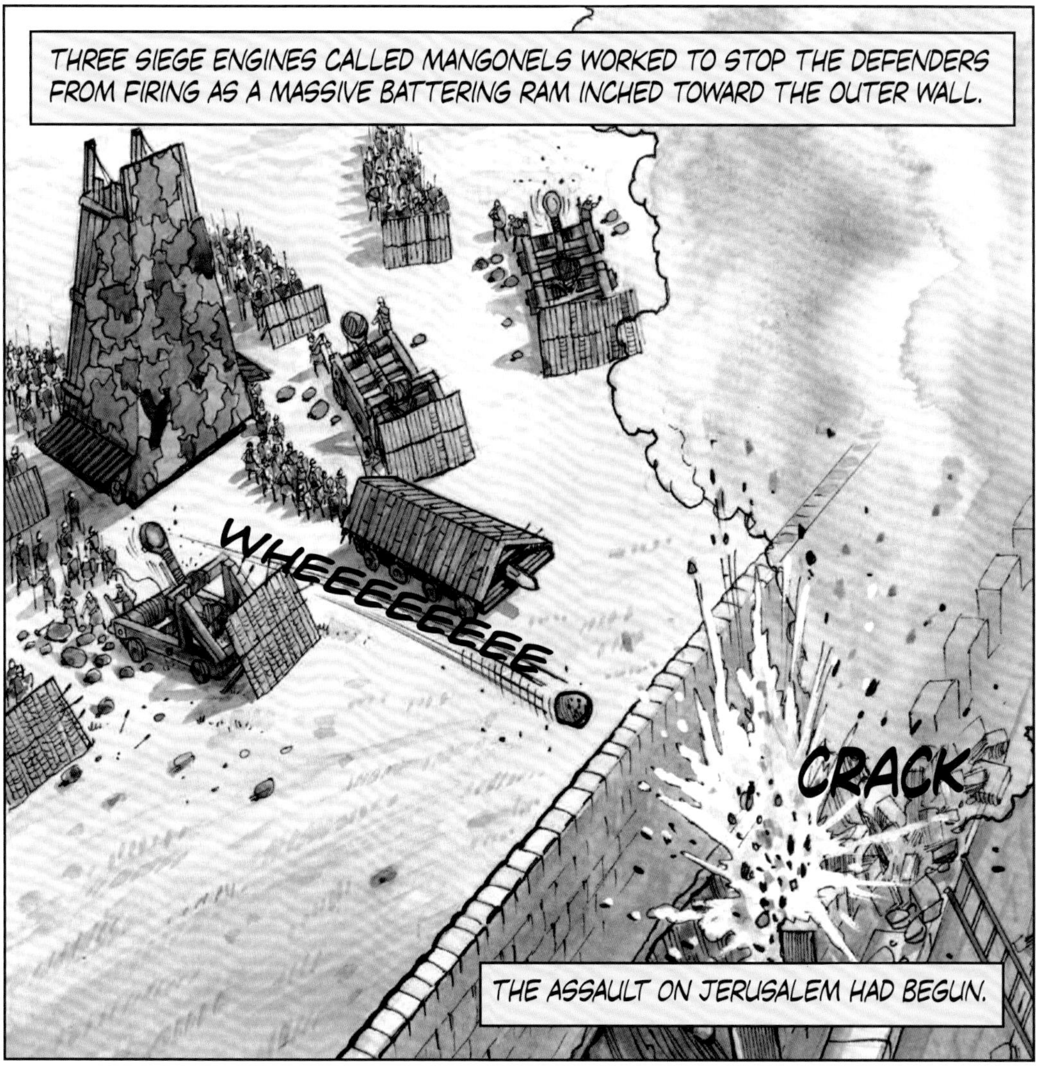
THREE SIEGE ENGINES CALLED MANGONELS WORKED TO STOP THE DEFENDERS FROM FIRING AS A MASSIVE BATTERING RAM INCHED TOWARD THE OUTER WALL.
WHEEEEEEEEEE
CRACK
THE ASSAULT ON JERUSALEM HAD BEGUN.

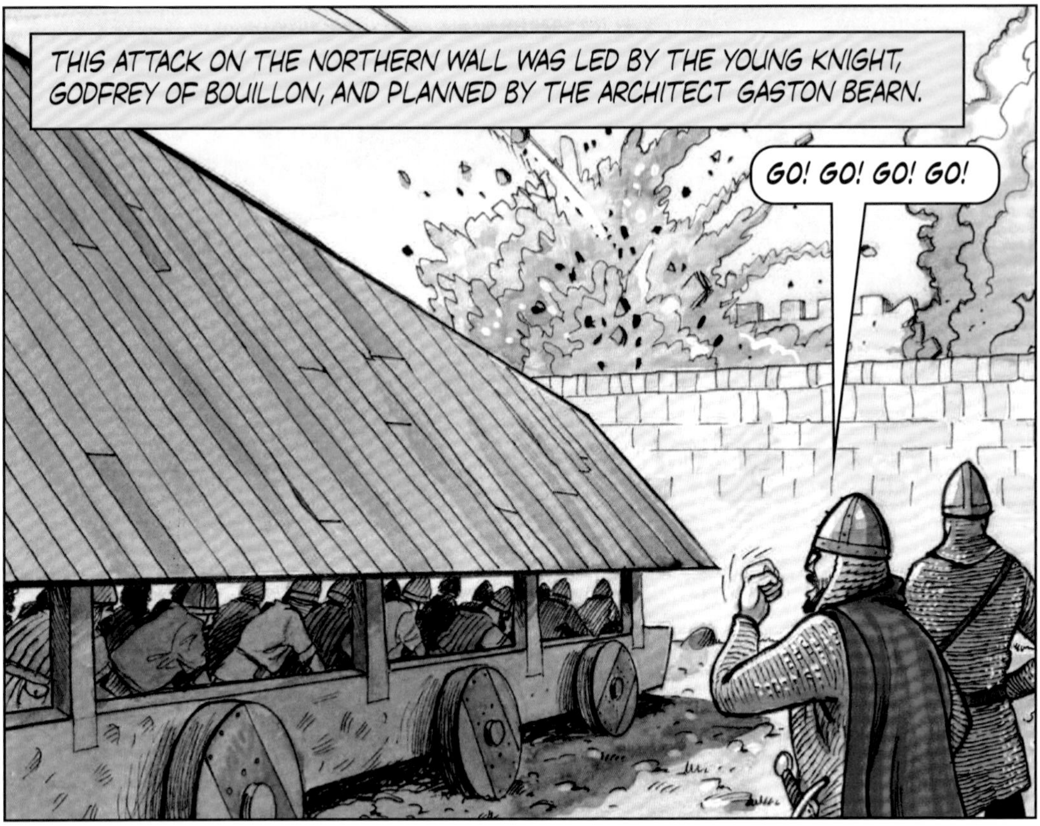
THIS ATTACK ON THE NORTHERN WALL WAS LED BY THE YOUNG KNIGHT, GODFREY OF BOUILLON, AND PLANNED BY THE ARCHITECT GASTON BEARN.
GO! GO! GO! GO!

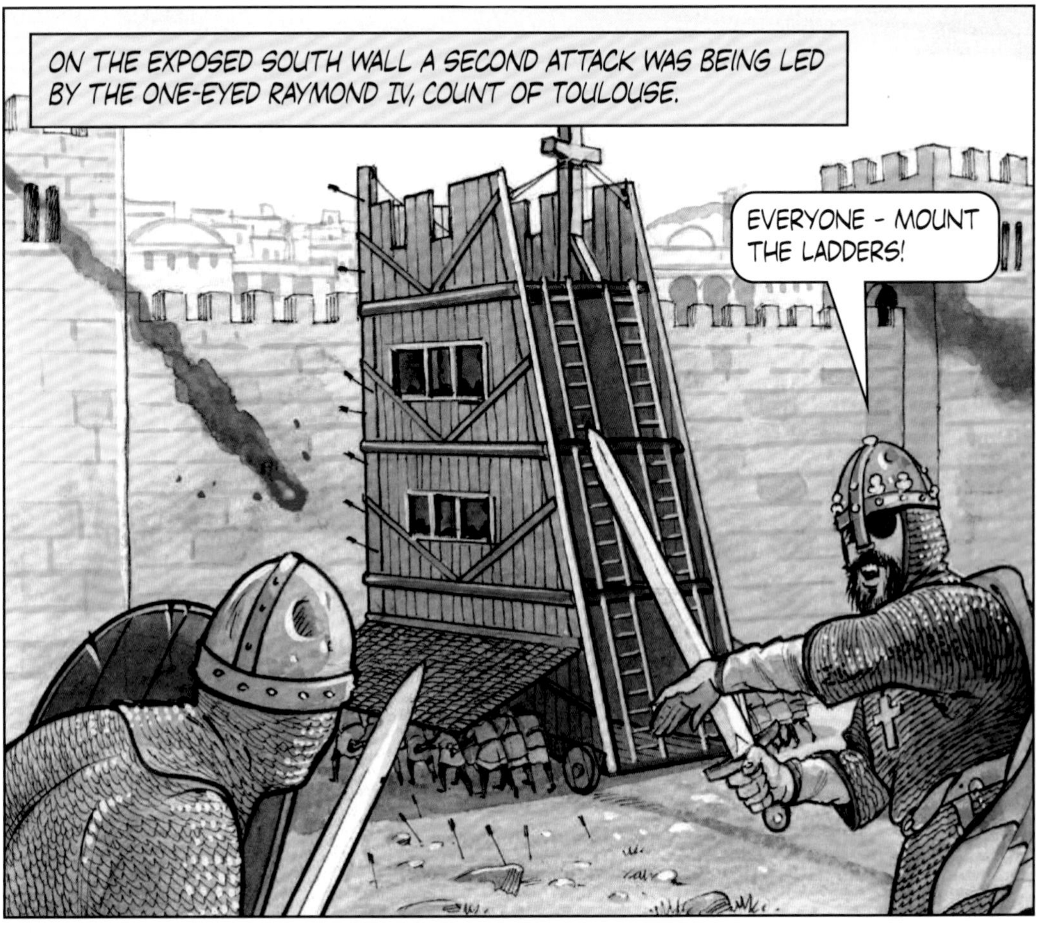
ON THE EXPOSED SOUTH WALL A SECOND ATTACK WAS BEING LED BY THE ONE-EYED RAYMOND IV, COUNT OF TOULOUSE.
EVERYONE - MOUNT THE LADDERS!

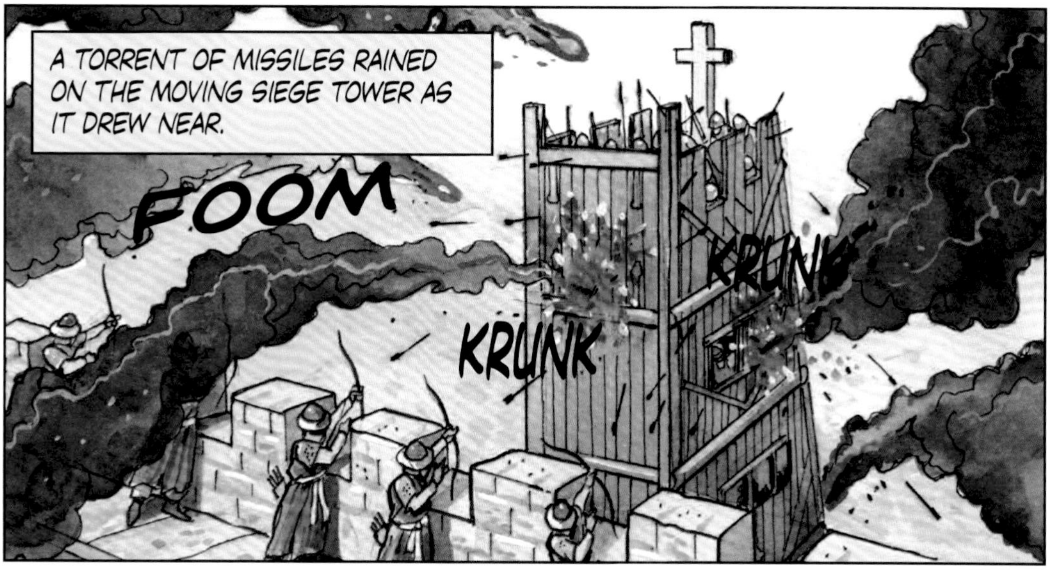
A TORRENT OF MISSILES RAINED ON THE MOVING SIEGE TOWER AS IT DREW NEAR.
FOOM
KRUNK
KRUNK

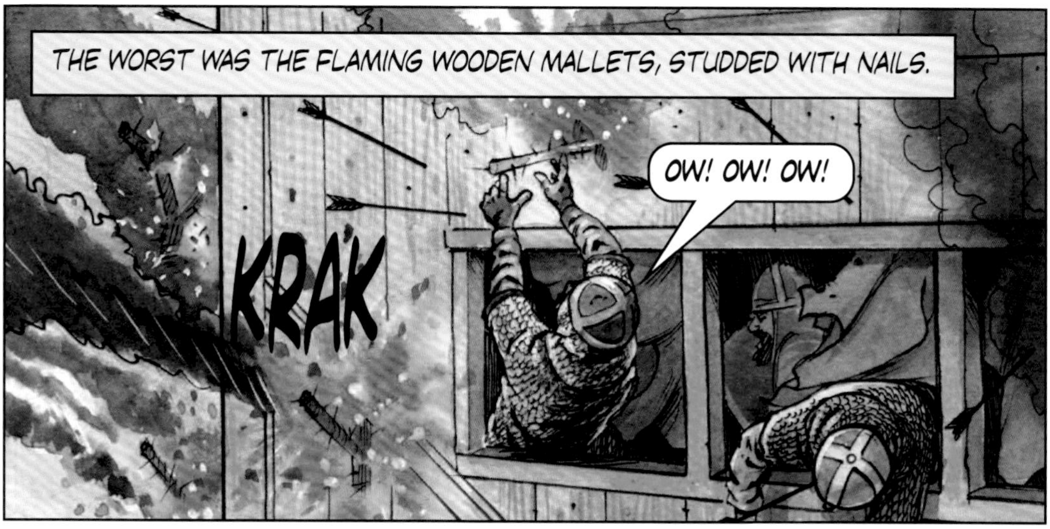
THE WORST WAS THE FLAMING WOODEN MALLETS, STUDDED WITH NAILS.
KRAK
OW! OW! OW!

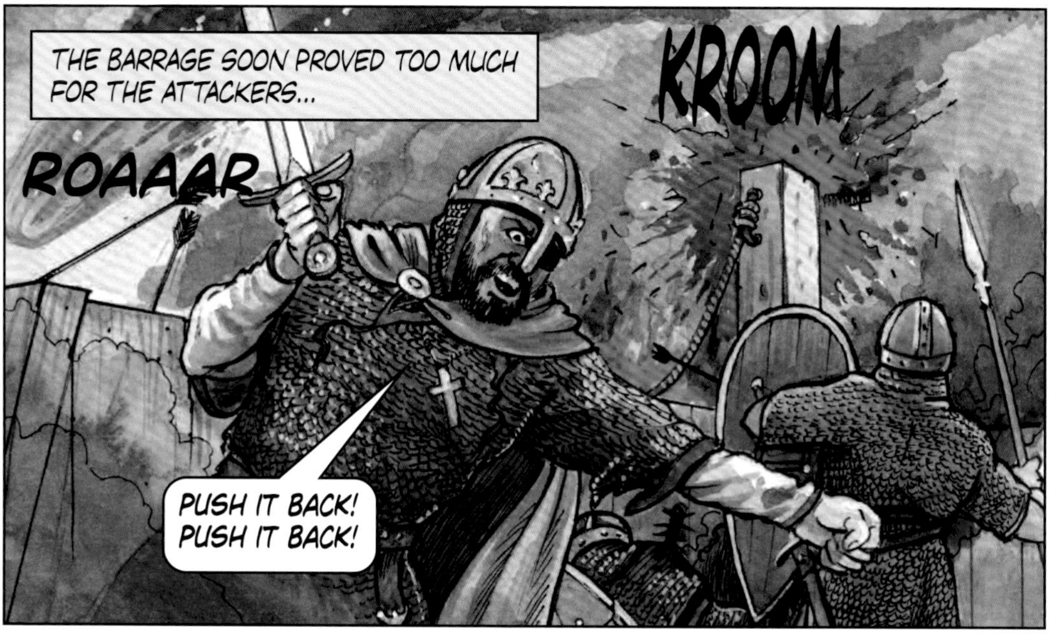
THE BARRAGE SOON PROVED TOO MUCH FOR THE ATTACKERS...
KROOM
ROAAAR
PUSH IT BACK! PUSH IT BACK!

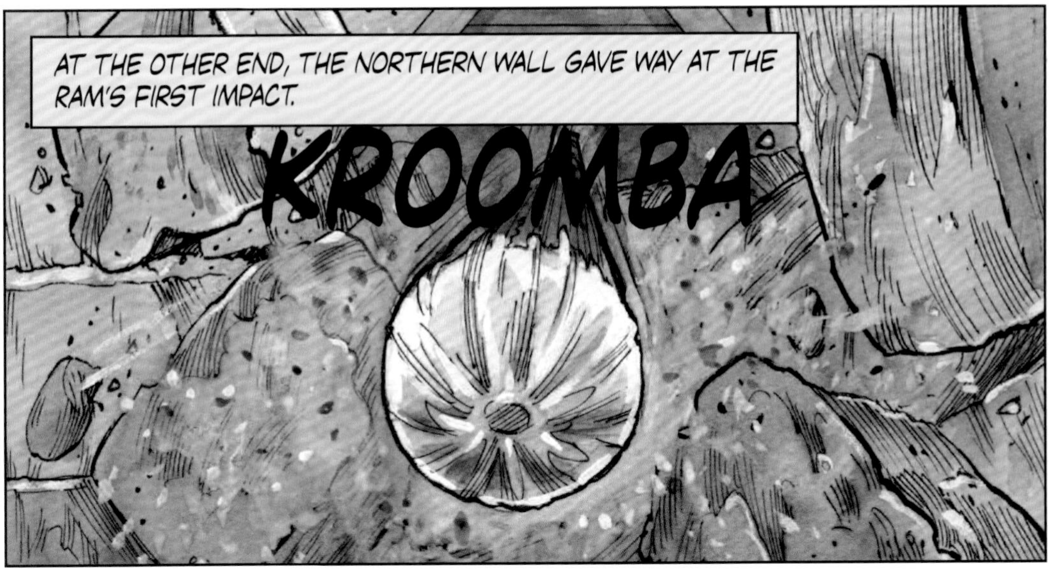
AT THE OTHER END, THE NORTHERN WALL GAVE WAY AT THE RAM'S FIRST IMPACT.
KROOMBA

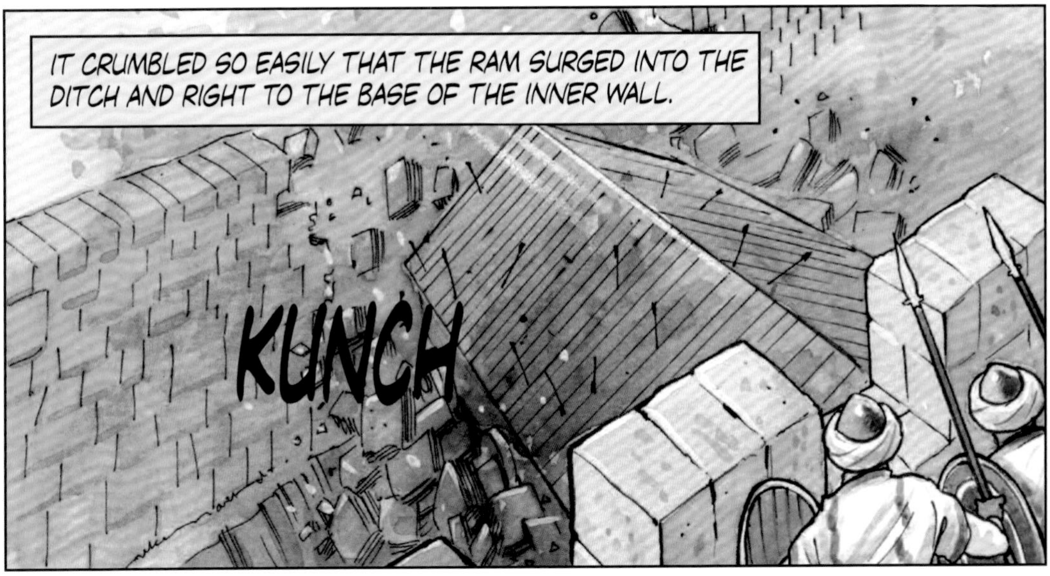
IT CRUMBLED SO EASILY THAT THE RAM SURGED INTO THE DITCH AND RIGHT TO THE BASE OF THE INNER WALL.
KUNCH

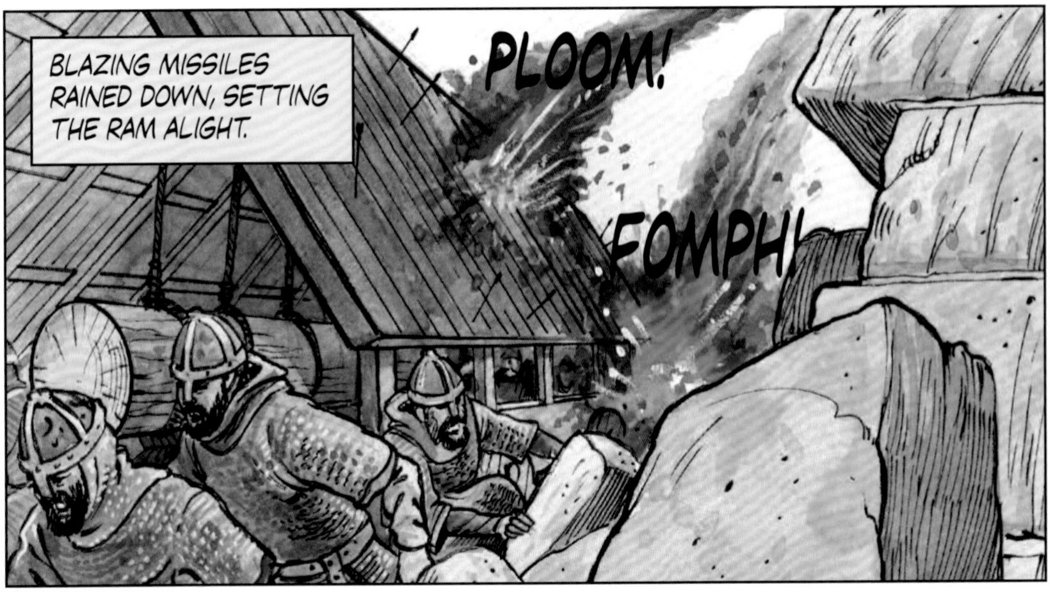
BLAZING MISSILES RAINED DOWN, SETTING THE RAM ALIGHT.
PLOOM!
FOMPH!

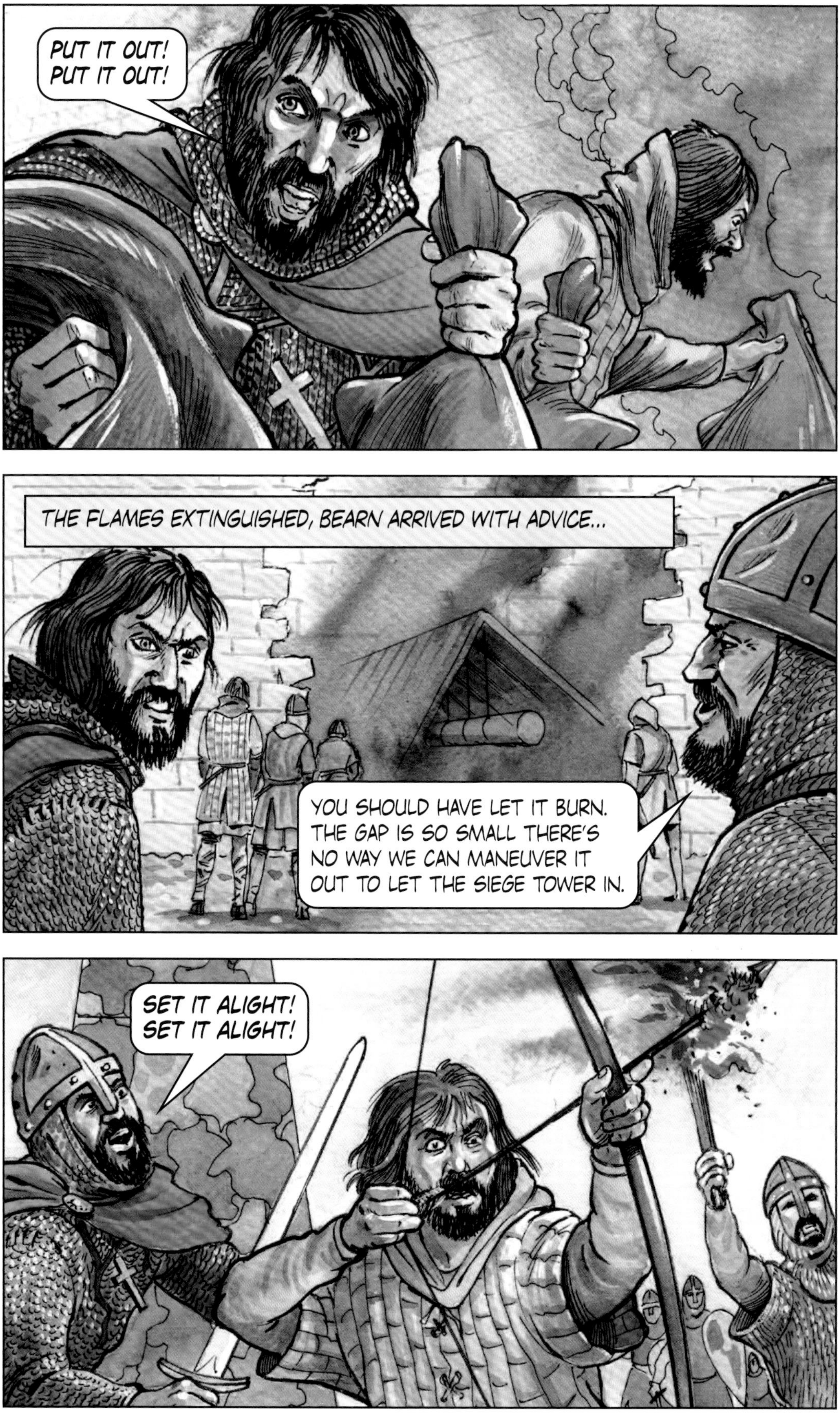
PUT IT OUT! PUT IT OUT!
THE FLAMES EXTINGUISHED, BEARN ARRIVED WITH ADVICE...
YOU SHOULD HAVE LET IT BURN. THE GAP IS SO SMALL THERE'S NO WAY WE CAN MANEUVER IT OUT TO LET THE SIEGE TOWER IN.
SET IT ALIGHT! SET IT ALIGHT!

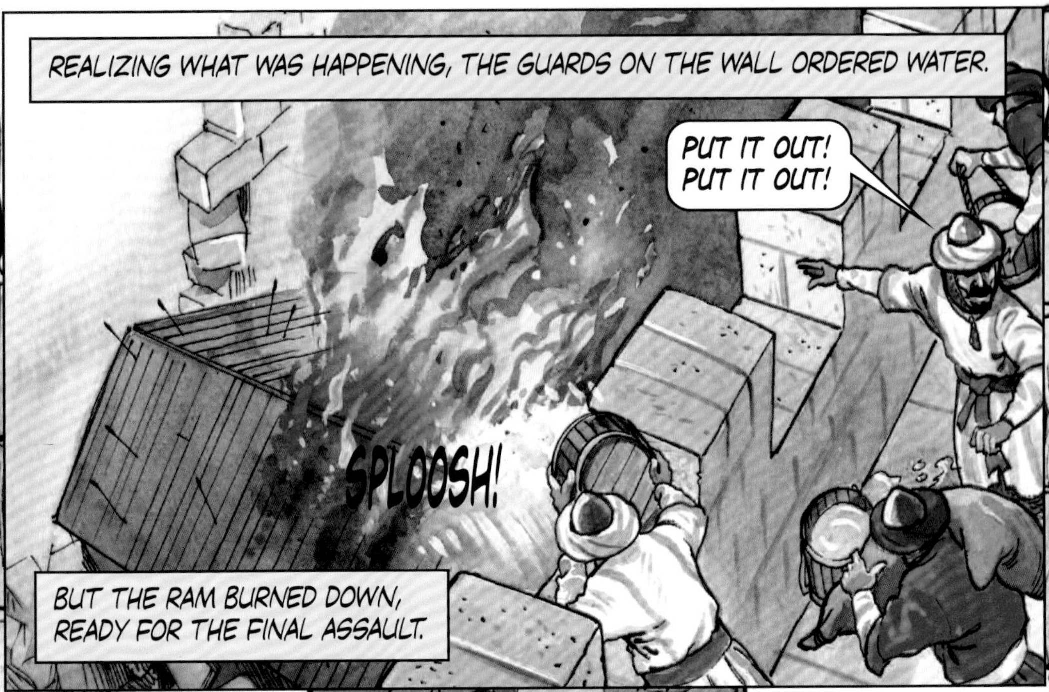
REALIZING WHAT WAS HAPPENING, THE GUARDS ON THE WALL ORDERED WATER.
PUT IT OUT! PUT IT OUT!
SPLOOSH!
BUT THE RAM BURNED DOWN, READY FOR THE FINAL ASSAULT.

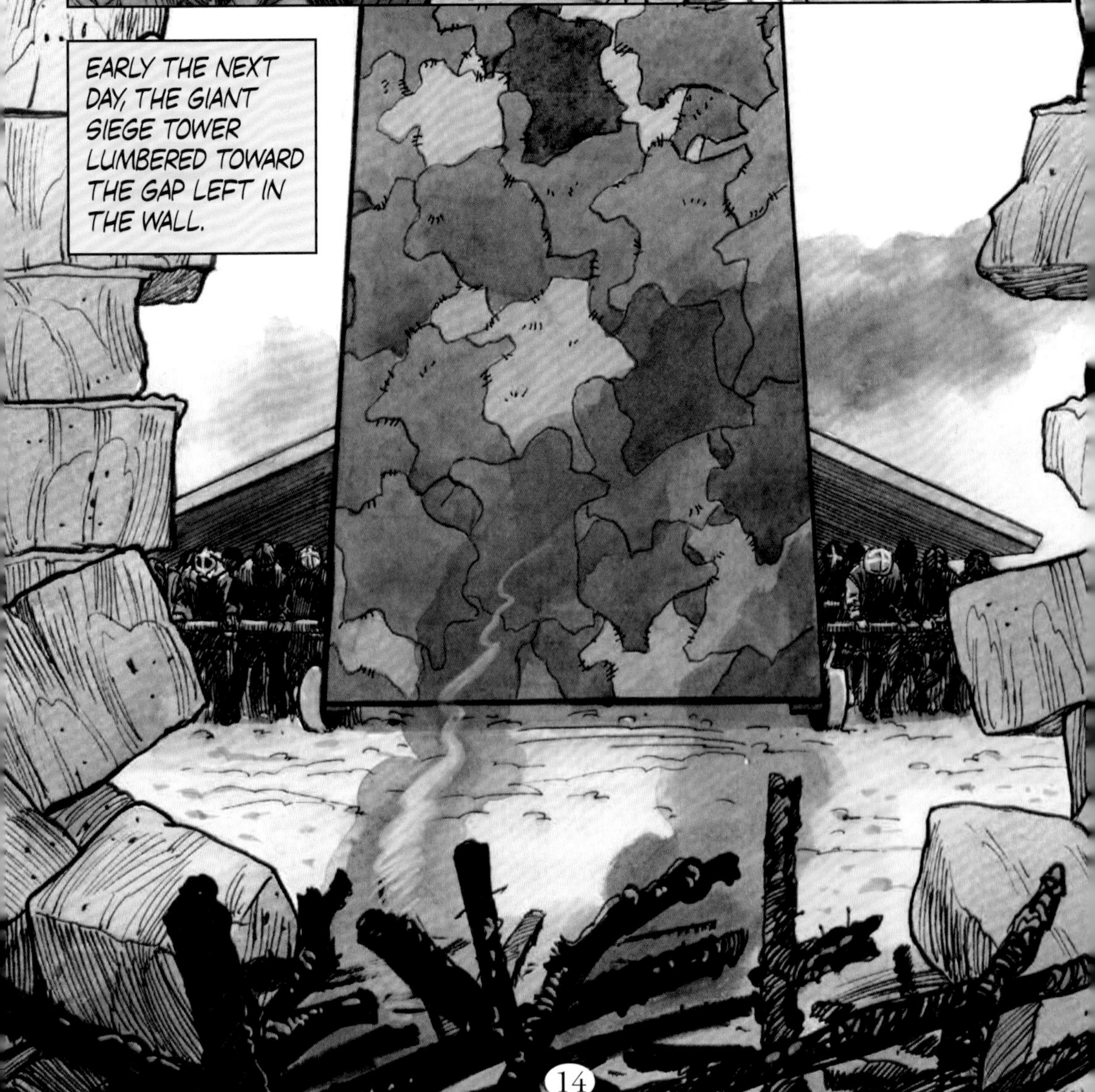
EARLY THE NEXT DAY, THE GIANT SIEGE TOWER LUMBERED TOWARD THE GAP LEFT IN THE WALL.

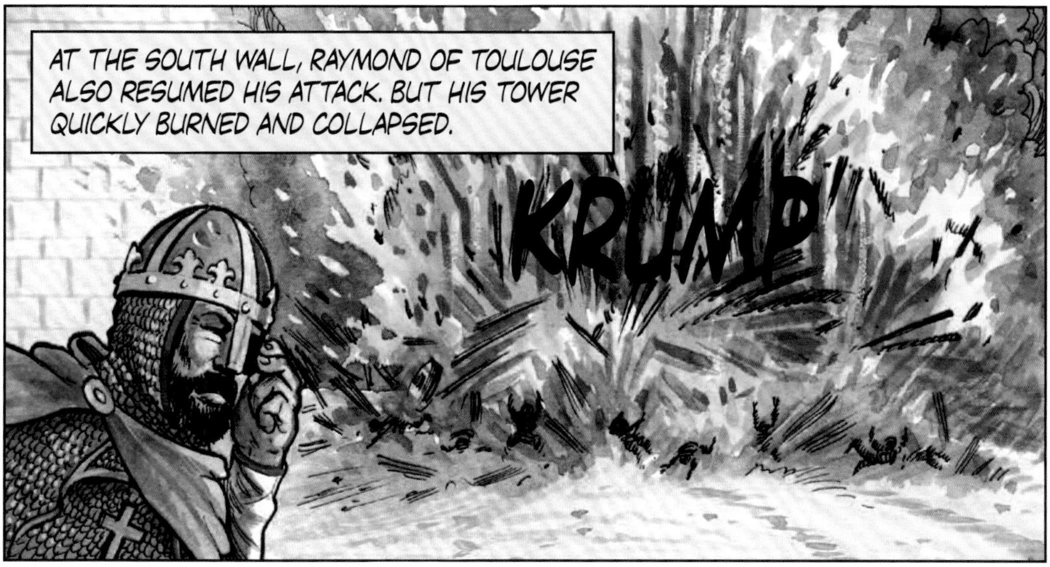
AT THE SOUTH WALL, RAYMOND OF TOULOUSE ALSO RESUMED HIS ATTACK. BUT HIS TOWER QUICKLY BURNED AND COLLAPSED.
KRUMP

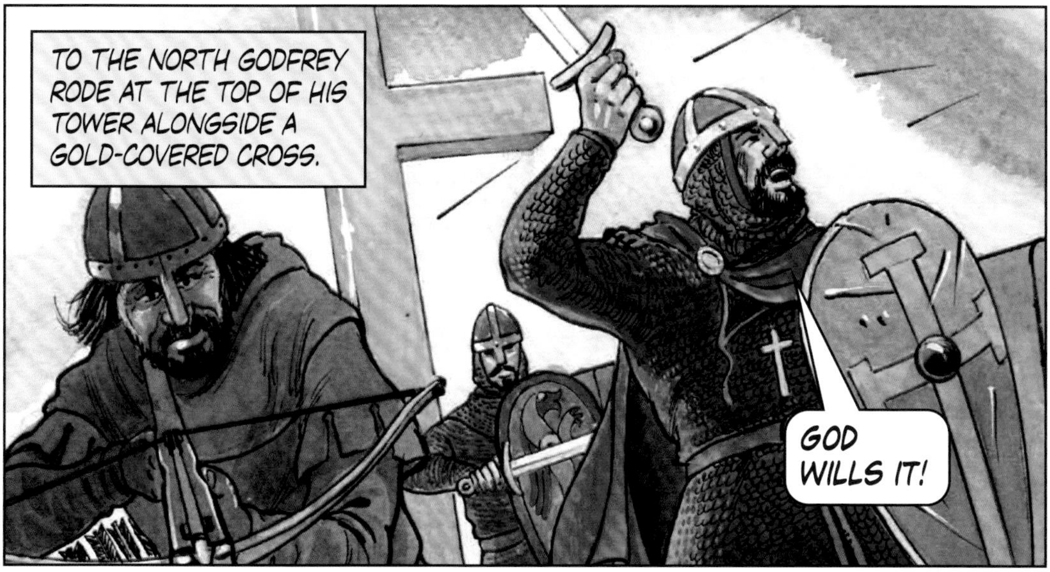
TO THE NORTH GODFREY RODE AT THE TOP OF HIS TOWER ALONGSIDE A GOLD-COVERED CROSS.
GOD WILLS IT!

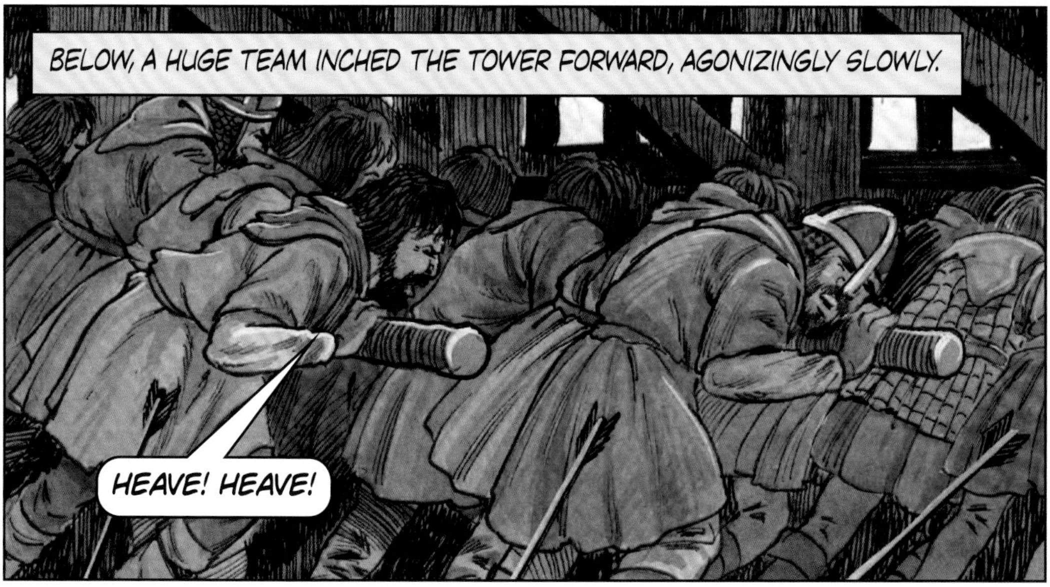
BELOW, A HUGE TEAM INCHED THE TOWER FORWARD, AGONIZINGLY SLOWLY.
HEAVE! HEAVE!

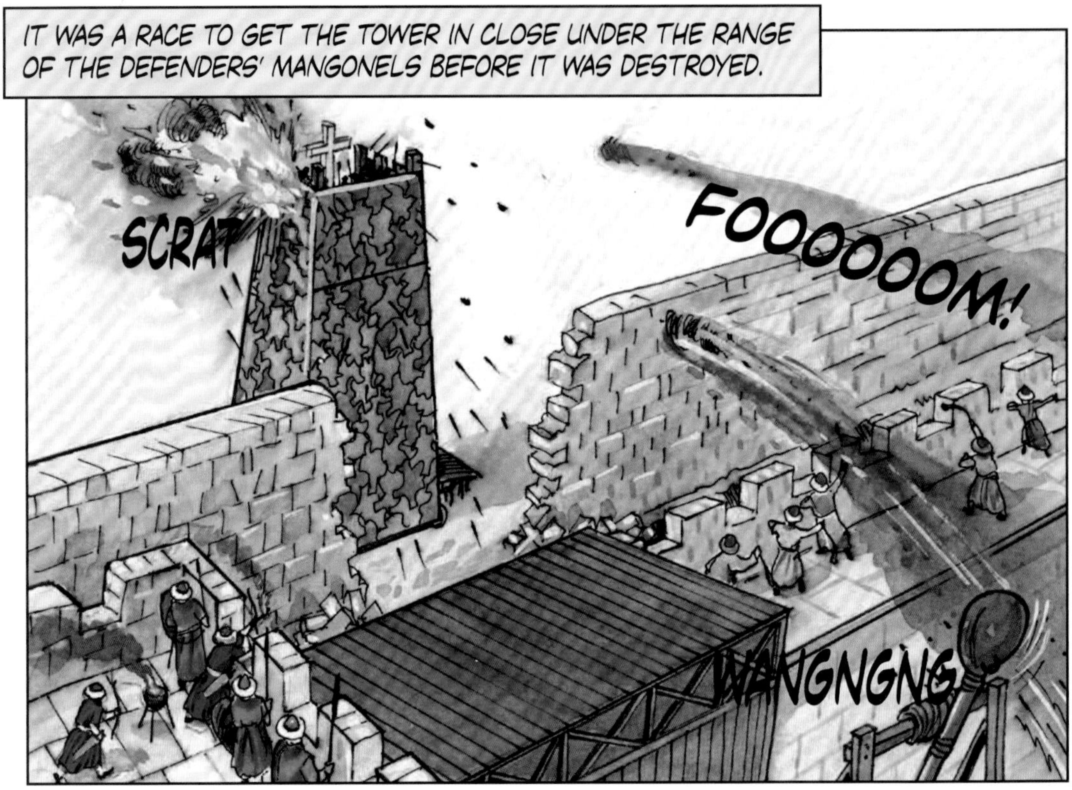
IT WAS A RACE TO GET THE TOWER IN CLOSE UNDER THE RANGE OF THE DEFENDERS' MANGONELS BEFORE IT WAS DESTROYED.
SCRAT
FOOOOOOM!
WANGNGNG

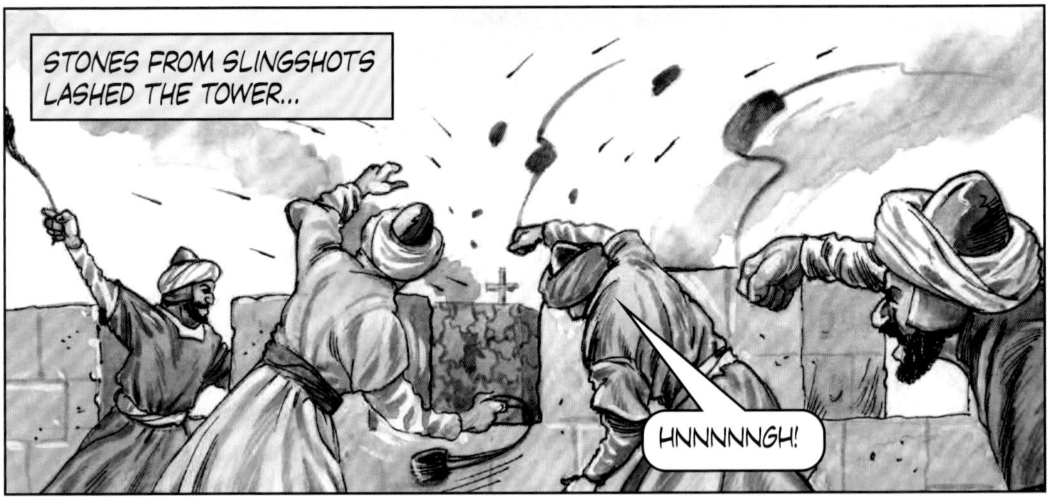
STONES FROM SLINGSHOTS LASHED THE TOWER...
HNNNNNGH!

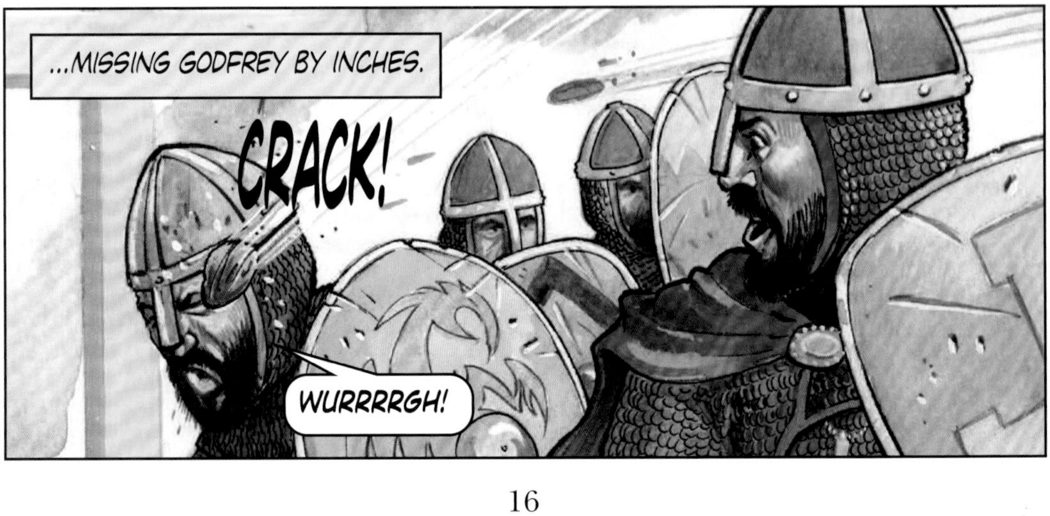
...MISSING GODFREY BY INCHES.
CRACK!
WURRRRGH!

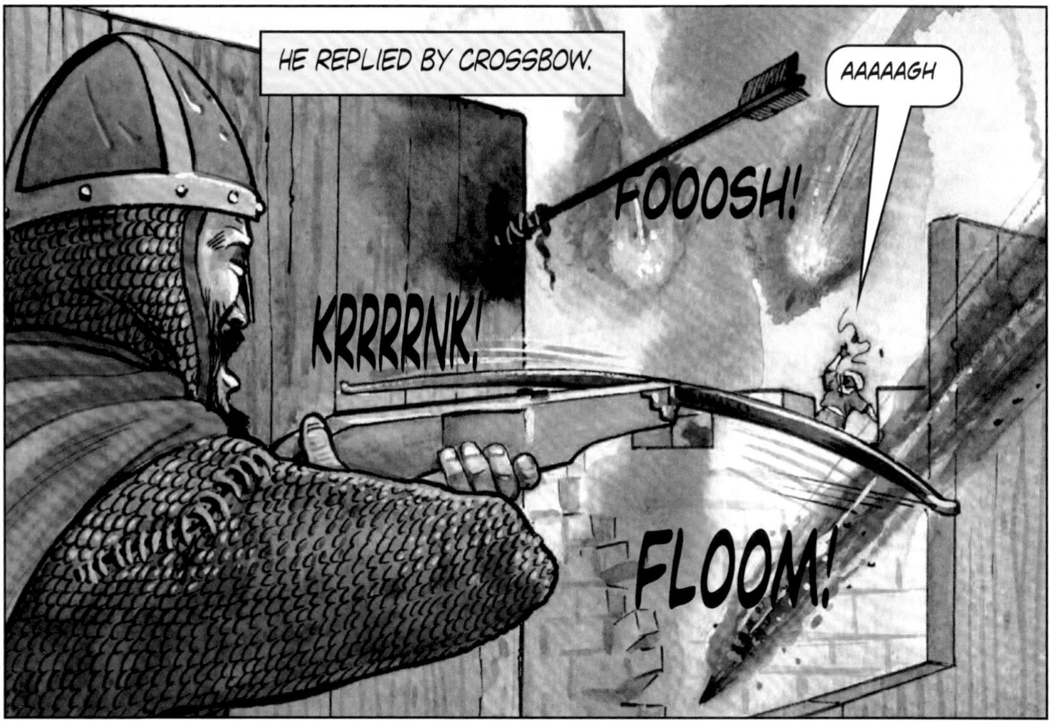
HE REPLIED BY CROSSBOW.
AAAAAGH
FOOOSH!
KRRRRNK!
FLOOM!

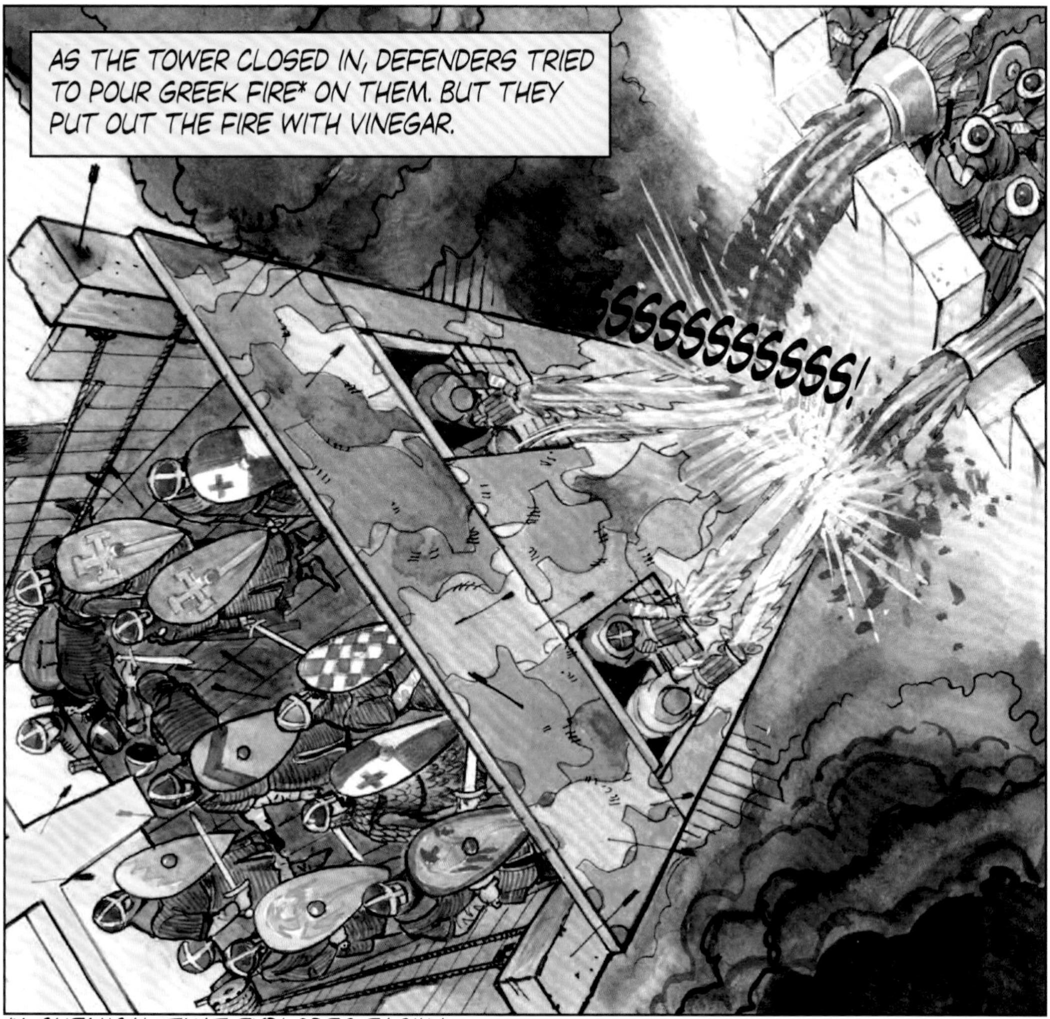
AS THE TOWER CLOSED IN, DEFENDERS TRIED TO POUR GREEK FIRE* ON THEM. BUT THEY PUT OUT THE FIRE WITH VINEGAR.
SSSSSSSSSSSS!

*A CHEMICAL THAT EXPLODES EASILY

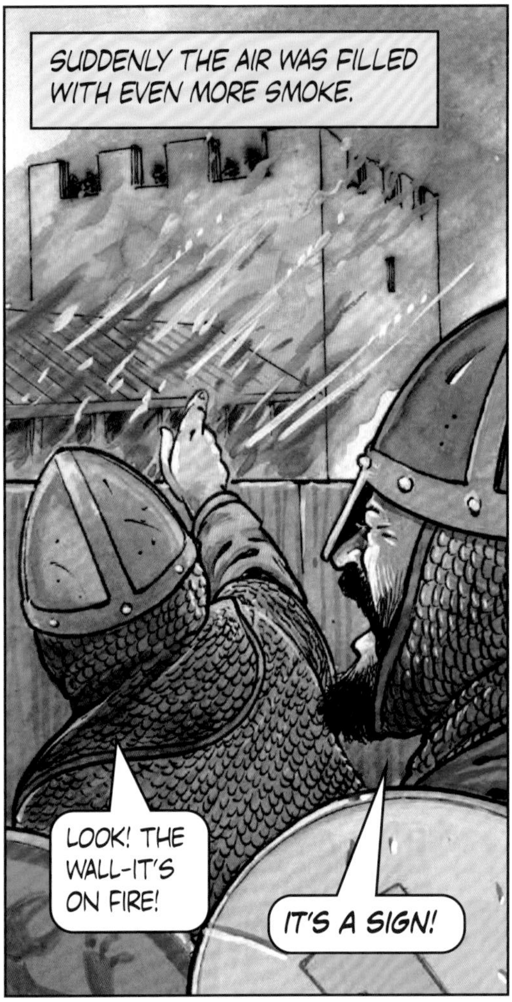
SUDDENLY THE AIR WAS FILLED WITH EVEN MORE SMOKE.
LOOK! THE WALL-IT'S ON FIRE!
IT'S A SIGN!

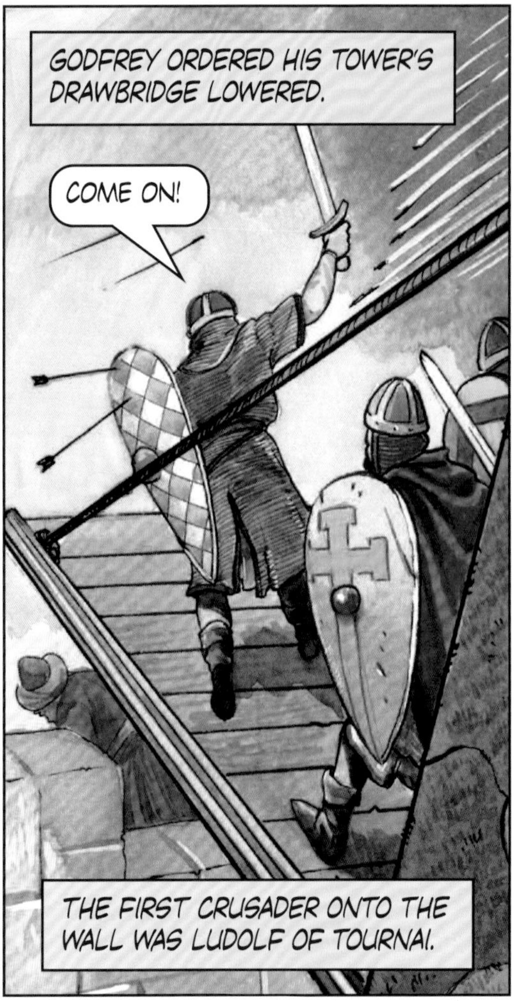
GODFREY ORDERED HIS TOWER'S DRAWBRIDGE LOWERED.
COME ON!
THE FIRST CRUSADER ONTO THE WALL WAS LUDOLF OF TOURNAI.

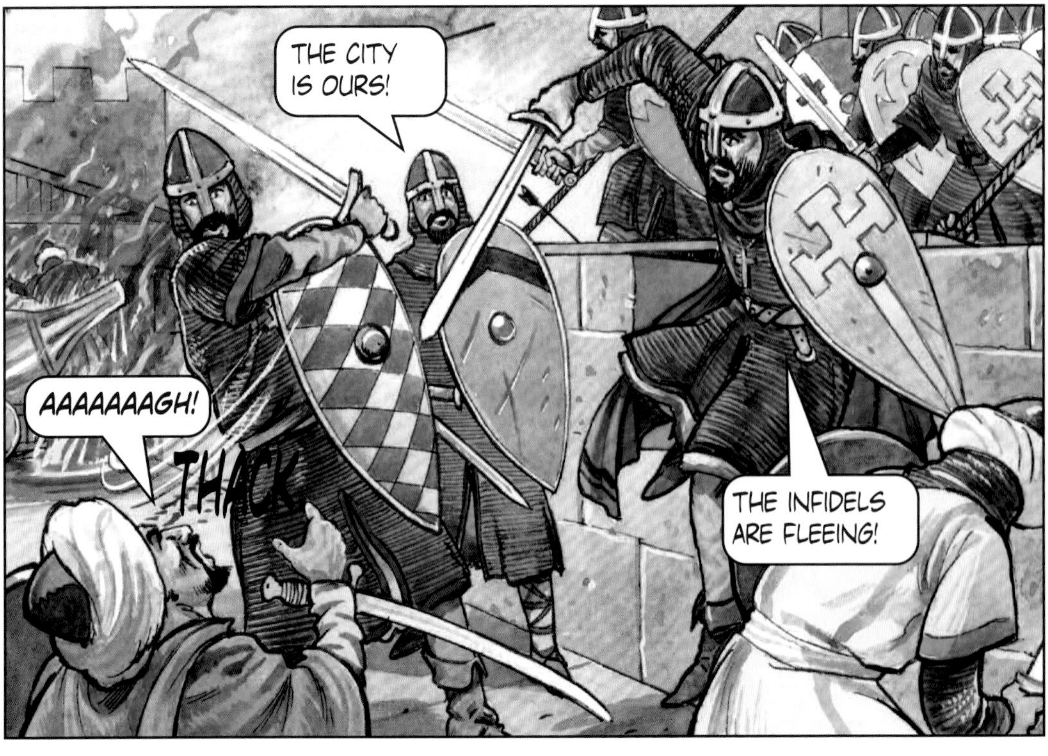
THE CITY IS OURS!
AAAAAAAGH!
THACK
THE INFIDELS ARE FLEEING!

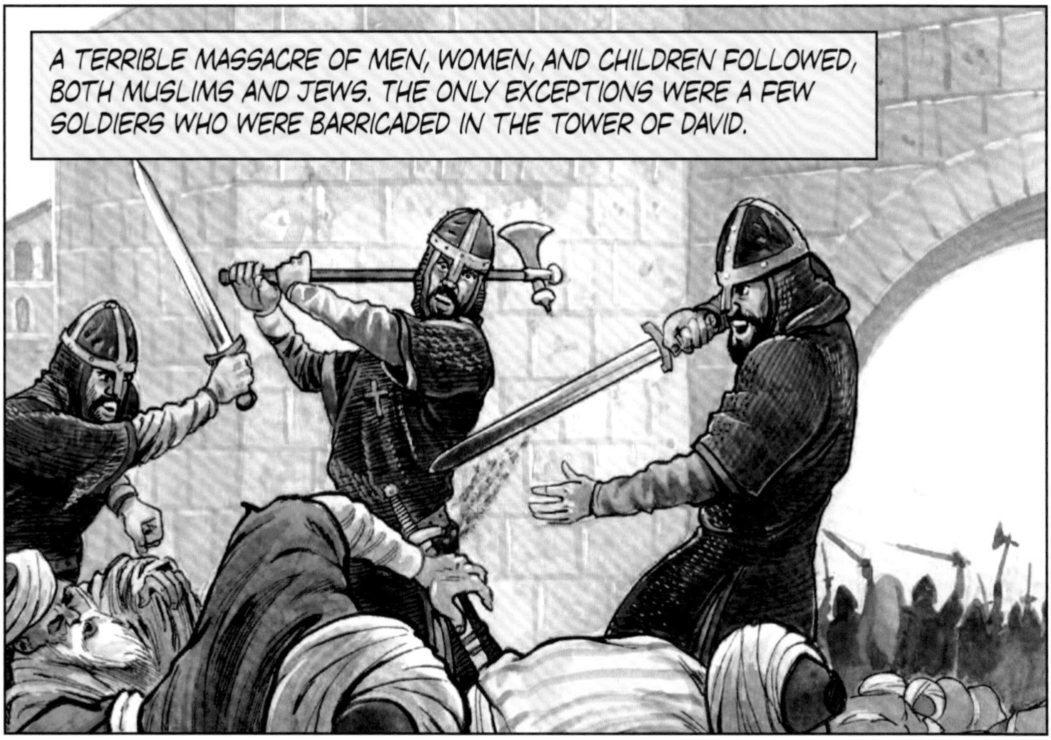
A TERRIBLE MASSACRE OF MEN, WOMEN, AND CHILDREN FOLLOWED, BOTH MUSLIMS AND JEWS. THE ONLY EXCEPTIONS WERE A FEW SOLDIERS WHO WERE BARRICADED IN THE TOWER OF DAVID.

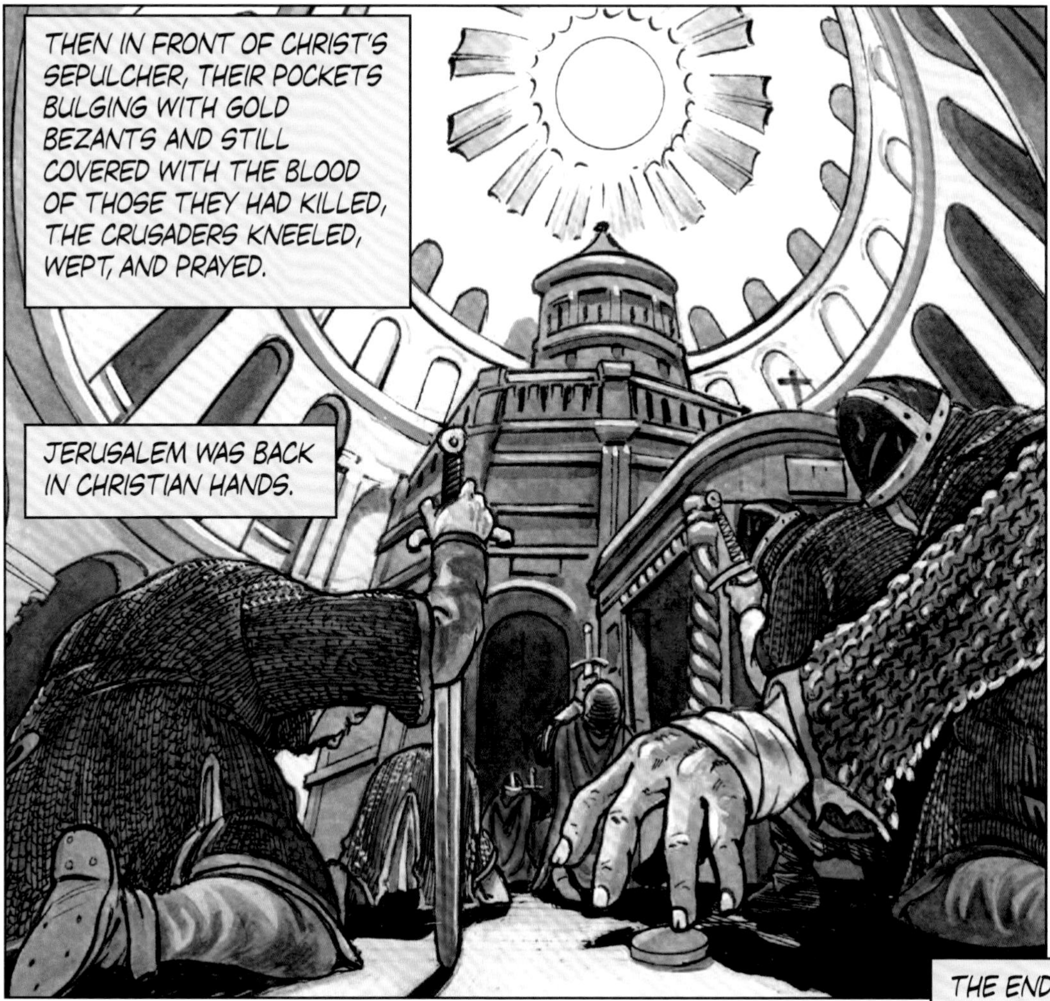
THEN IN FRONT OF CHRIST'S SEPULCHER, THEIR POCKETS BULGING WITH GOLD BEZANTS AND STILL COVERED WITH THE BLOOD OF THOSE THEY HAD KILLED, THE CRUSADERS KNEELED, WEPT, AND PRAYED.
JERUSALEM WAS BACK IN CHRISTIAN HANDS.

THE END

The Battle of Hattin

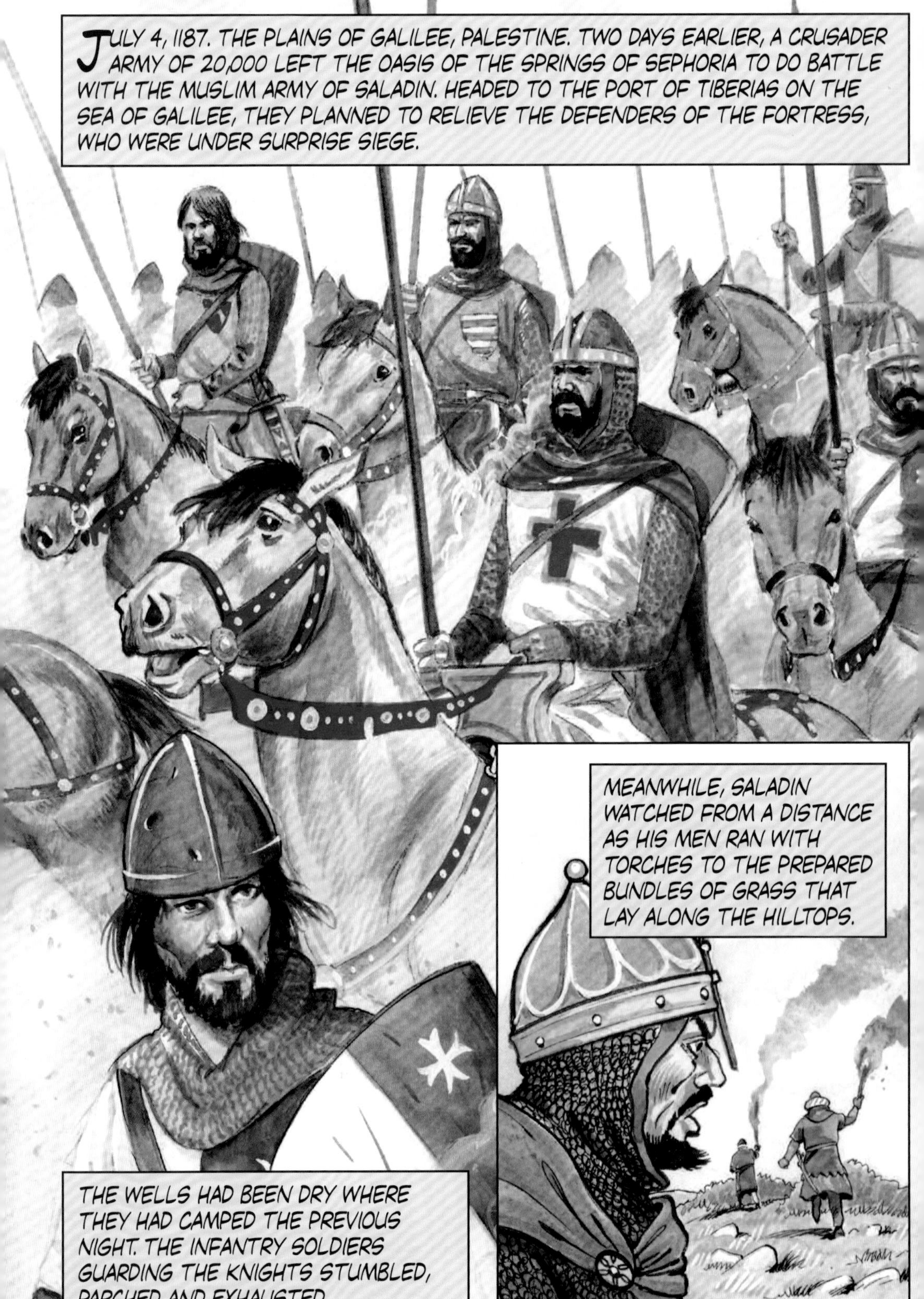
JULY 4, 1187. THE PLAINS OF GALILEE, PALESTINE. TWO DAYS EARLIER, A CRUSADER ARMY OF 20,000 LEFT THE OASIS OF THE SPRINGS OF SEPHORIA TO DO BATTLE WITH THE MUSLIM ARMY OF SALADIN. HEADED TO THE PORT OF TIBERIAS ON THE SEA OF GALILEE, THEY PLANNED TO RELIEVE THE DEFENDERS OF THE FORTRESS, WHO WERE UNDER SURPRISE SIEGE.
THE WELLS HAD BEEN DRY WHERE THEY HAD CAMPED THE PREVIOUS NIGHT. THE INFANTRY SOLDIERS GUARDING THE KNIGHTS STUMBLED, PARCHED AND EXHAUSTED.
MEANWHILE, SALADIN WATCHED FROM A DISTANCE AS HIS MEN RAN WITH TORCHES TO THE PREPARED BUNDLES OF GRASS THAT LAY ALONG THE HILLTOPS.

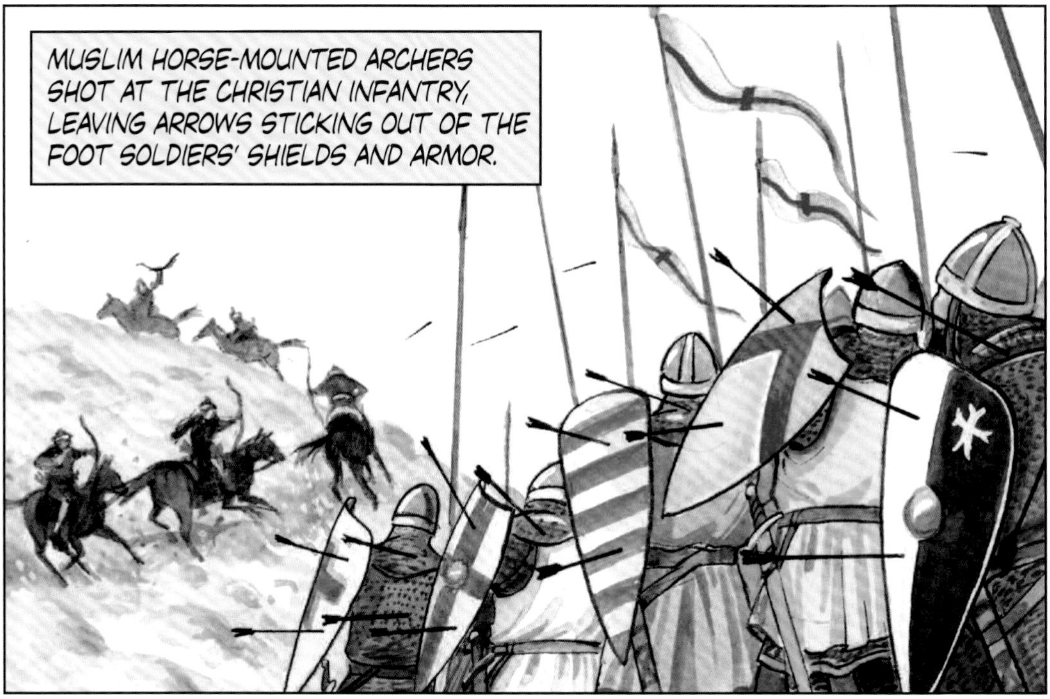
MUSLIM HORSE-MOUNTED ARCHERS SHOT AT THE CHRISTIAN INFANTRY, LEAVING ARROWS STICKING OUT OF THE FOOT SOLDIERS' SHIELDS AND ARMOR.

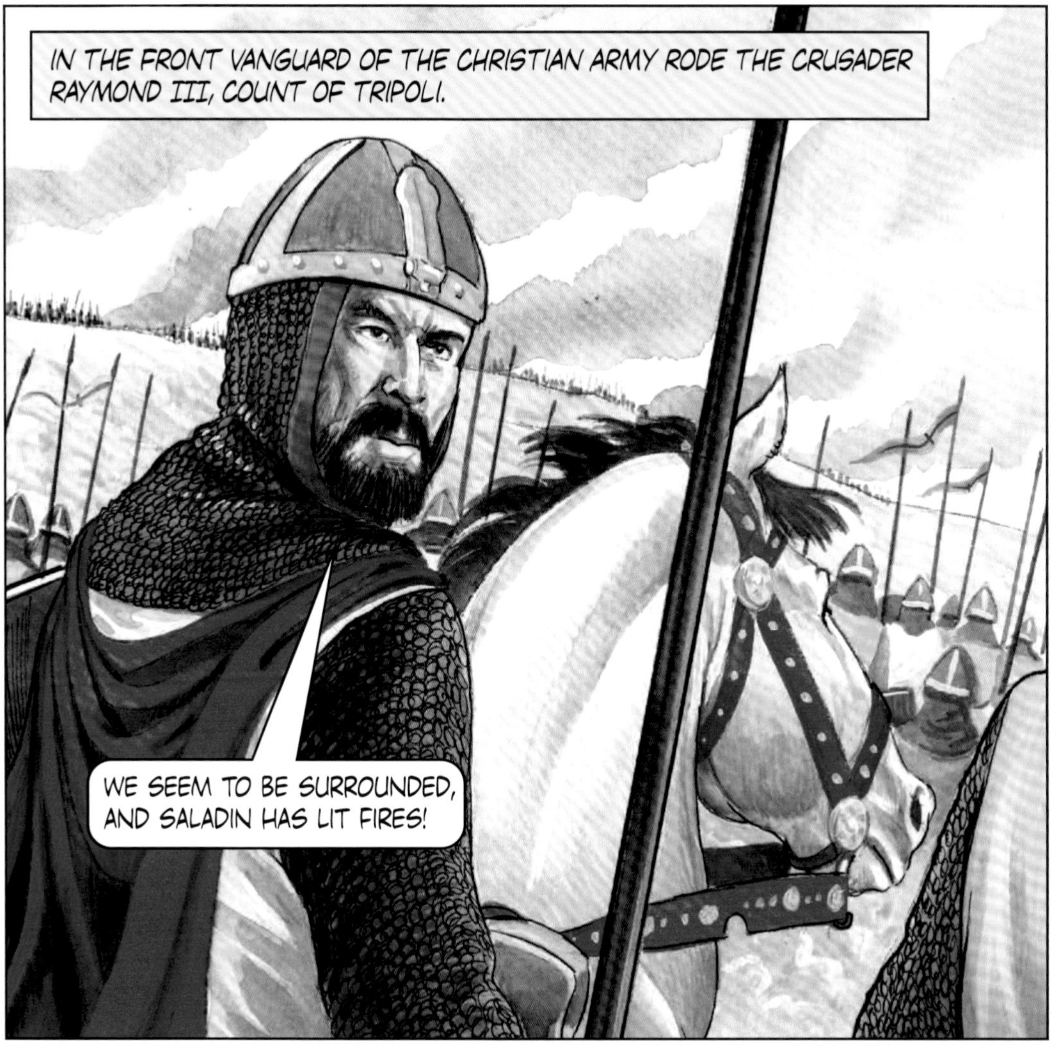
IN THE FRONT VANGUARD OF THE CHRISTIAN ARMY RODE THE CRUSADER RAYMOND III, COUNT OF TRIPOLI.
WE SEEM TO BE SURROUNDED, AND SALADIN HAS LIT FIRES!

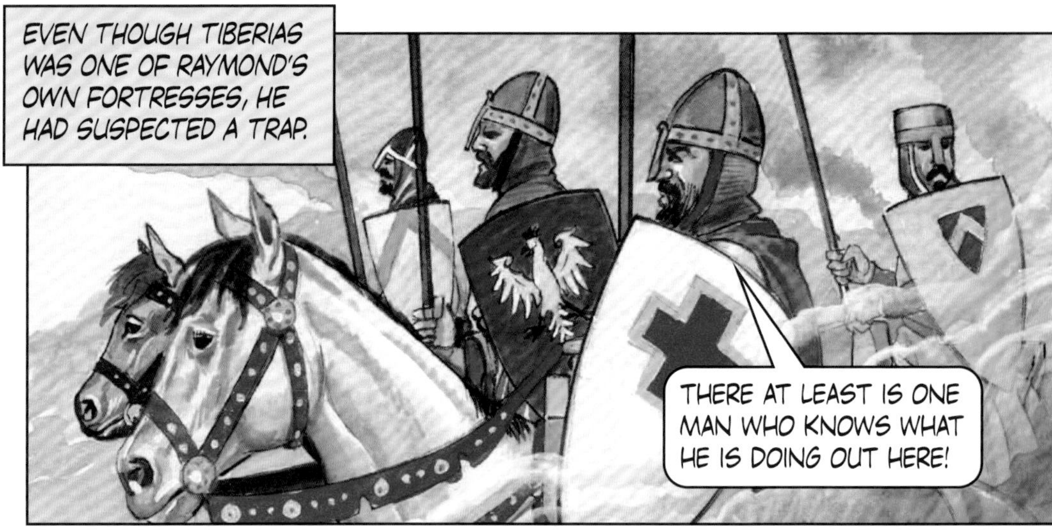
EVEN THOUGH TIBERIAS WAS ONE OF RAYMOND'S OWN FORTRESSES, HE HAD SUSPECTED A TRAP.
THERE AT LEAST IS ONE MAN WHO KNOWS WHAT HE IS DOING OUT HERE!

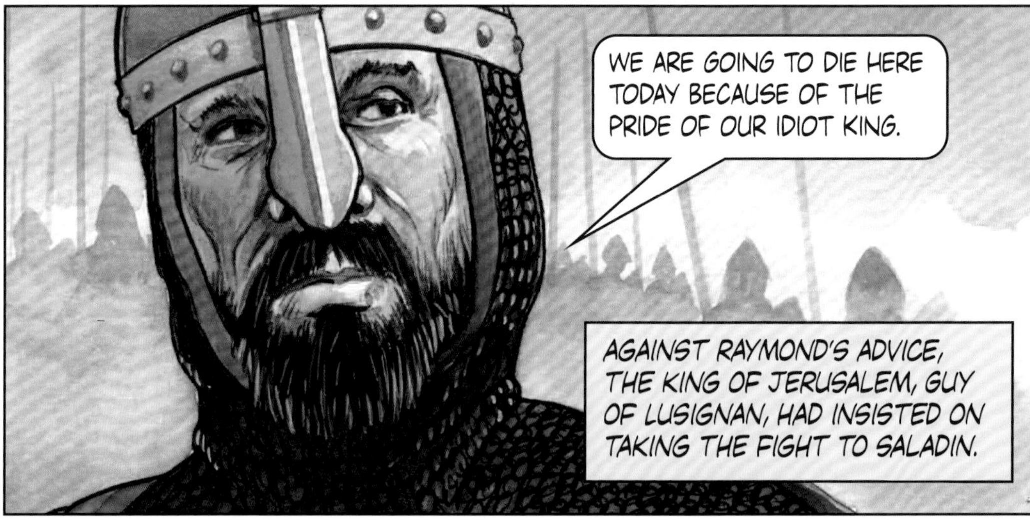
WE ARE GOING TO DIE HERE TODAY BECAUSE OF THE PRIDE OF OUR IDIOT KING.
AGAINST RAYMOND'S ADVICE, THE KING OF JERUSALEM, GUY OF LUSIGNAN, HAD INSISTED ON TAKING THE FIGHT TO SALADIN.

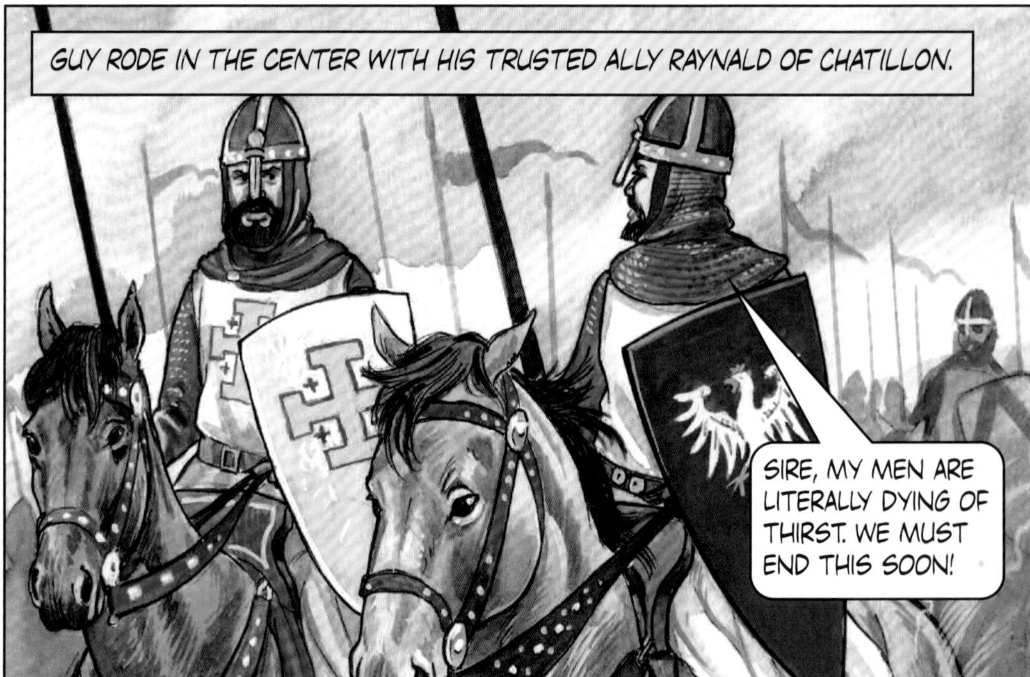
GUY RODE IN THE CENTER WITH HIS TRUSTED ALLY RAYNALD OF CHATILLON.
SIRE, MY MEN ARE LITERALLY DYING OF THIRST. WE MUST END THIS SOON!

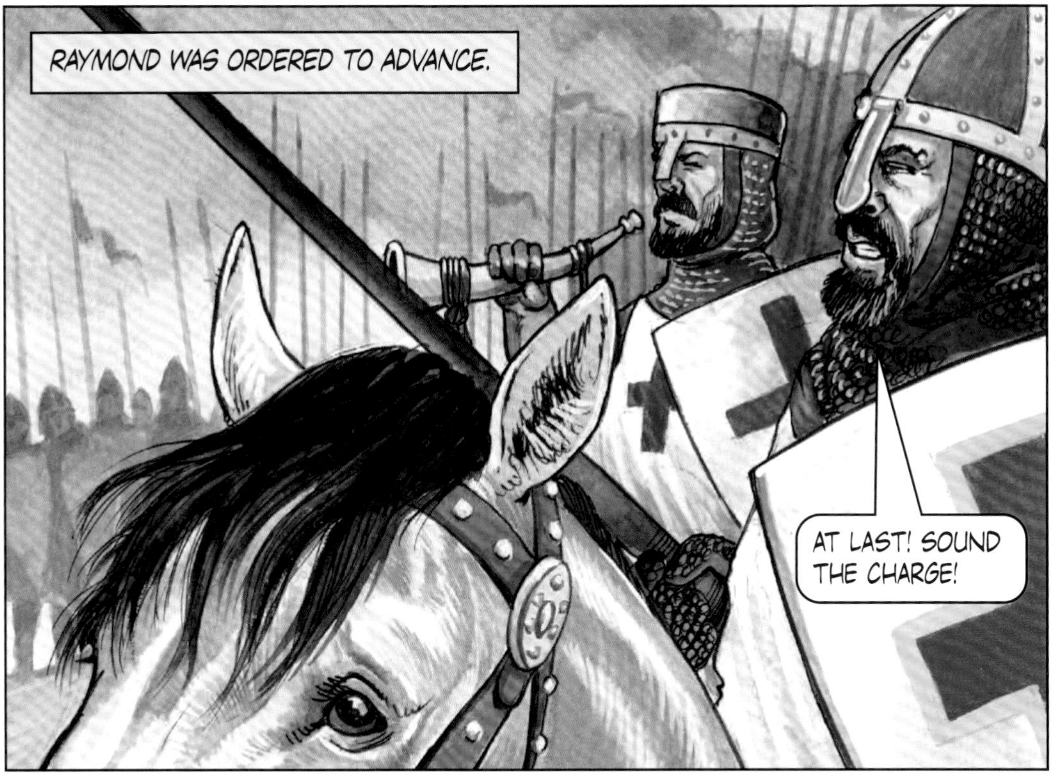
RAYMOND WAS ORDERED TO ADVANCE.
AT LAST! SOUND THE CHARGE!

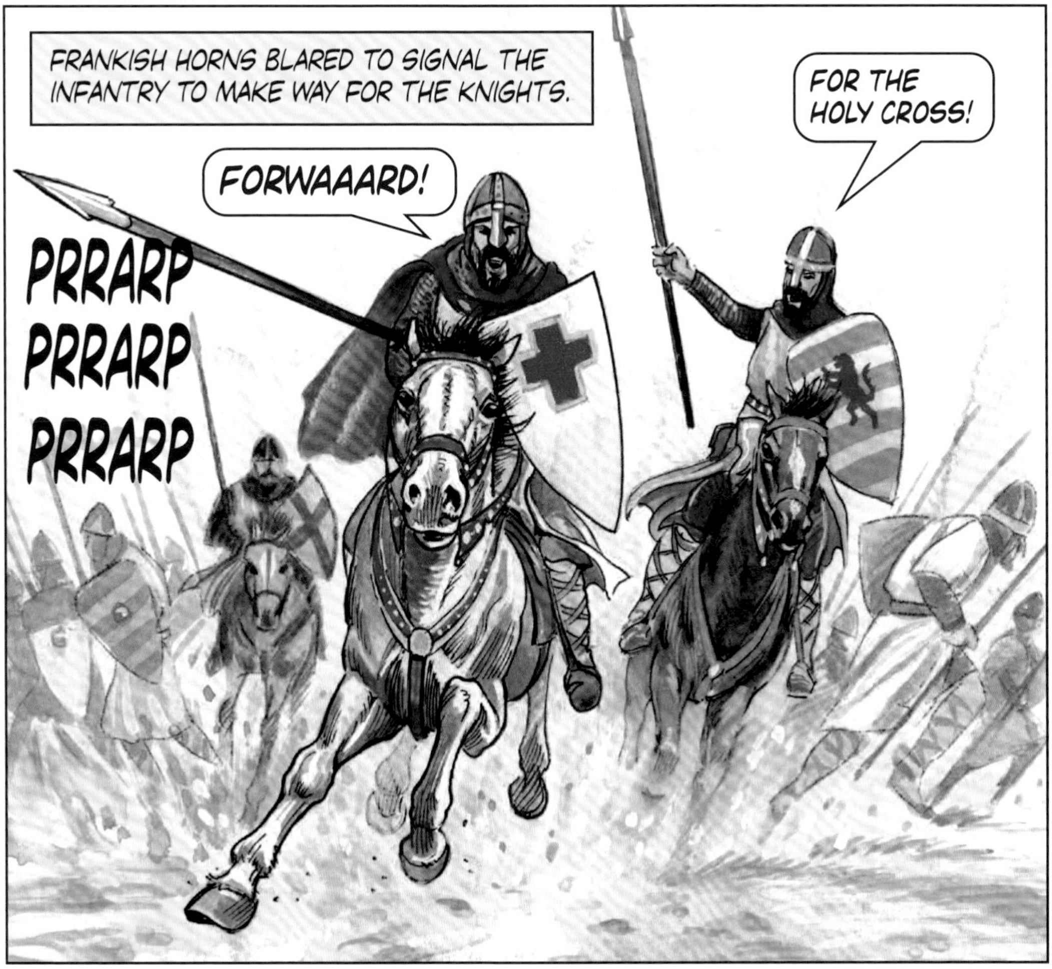
FRANKISH HORNS BLARED TO SIGNAL THE INFANTRY TO MAKE WAY FOR THE KNIGHTS.
FORWAAARD!
FOR THE HOLY CROSS!
PRRARP
PRRARP
PRRARP

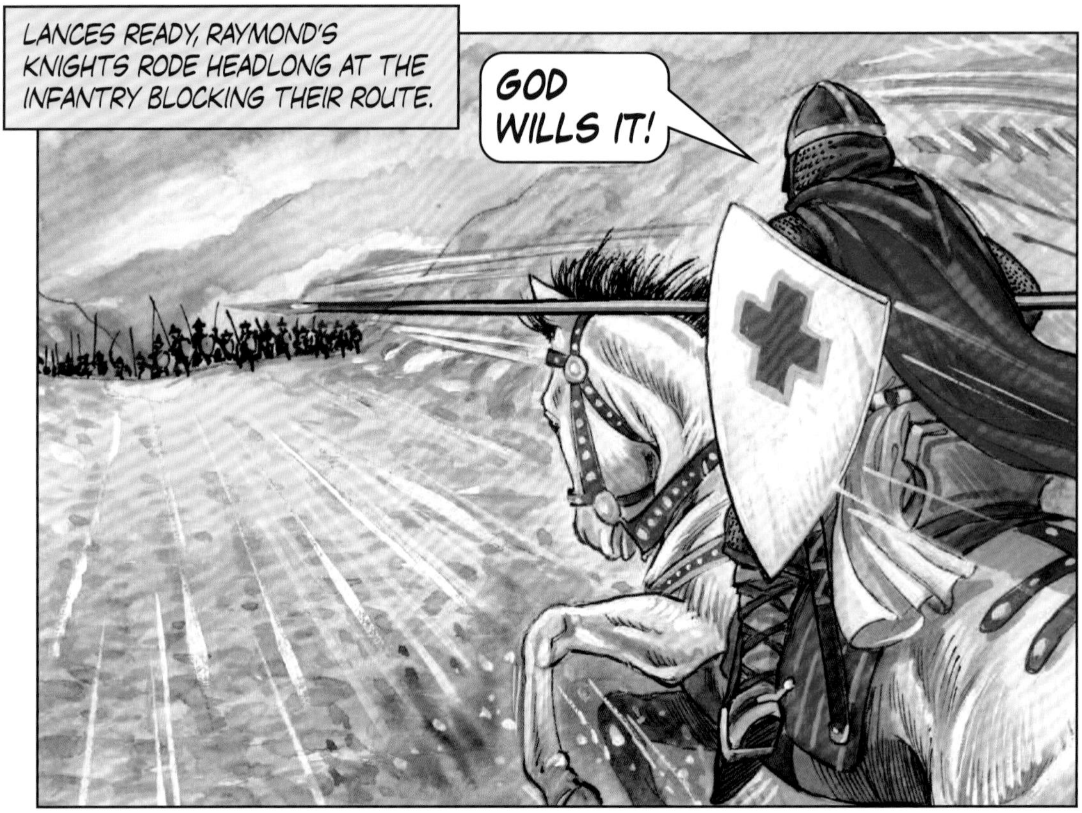
LANCES READY, RAYMOND'S KNIGHTS RODE HEADLONG AT THE INFANTRY BLOCKING THEIR ROUTE.
GOD WILLS IT!

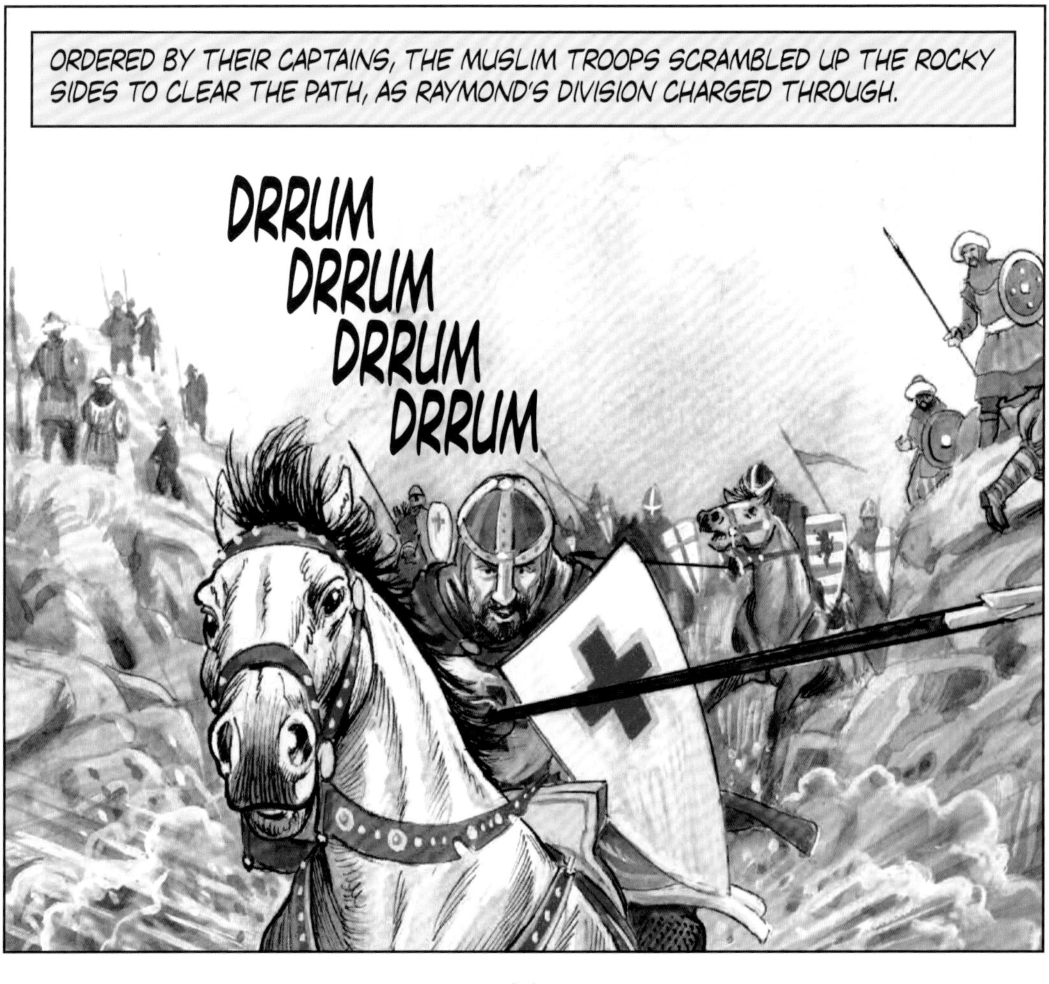
ORDERED BY THEIR CAPTAINS, THE MUSLIM TROOPS SCRAMBLED UP THE ROCKY SIDES TO CLEAR THE PATH, AS RAYMOND'S DIVISION CHARGED THROUGH.
DRRUM
DRRUM
DRRUM
DRRUM

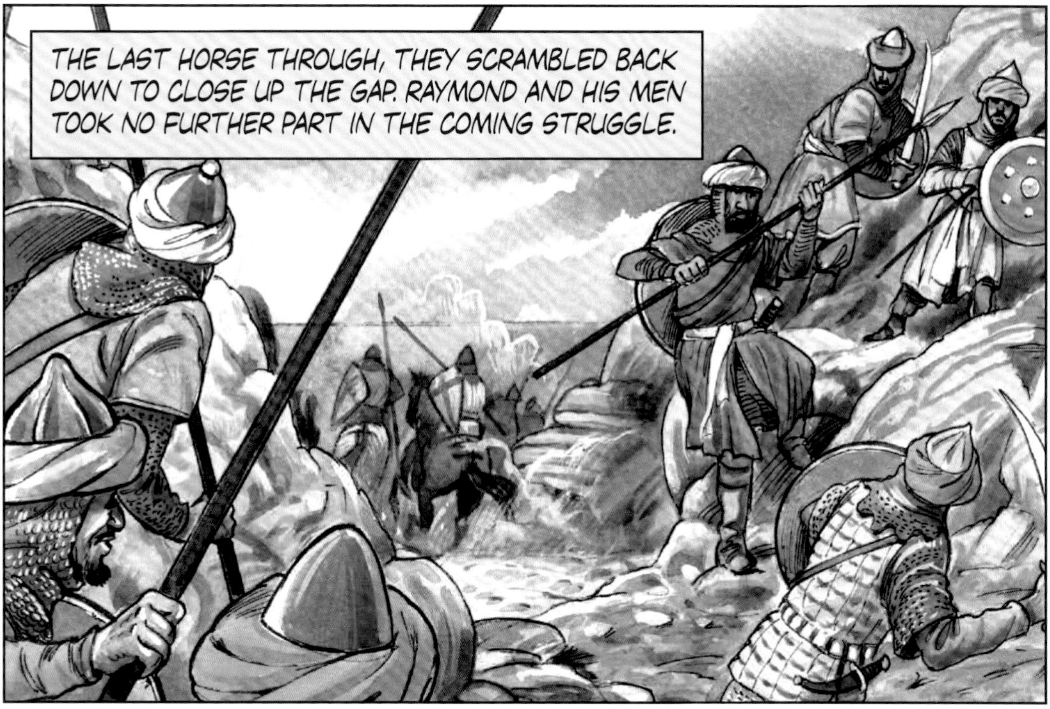
THE LAST HORSE THROUGH, THEY SCRAMBLED BACK DOWN TO CLOSE UP THE GAP. RAYMOND AND HIS MEN TOOK NO FURTHER PART IN THE COMING STRUGGLE.

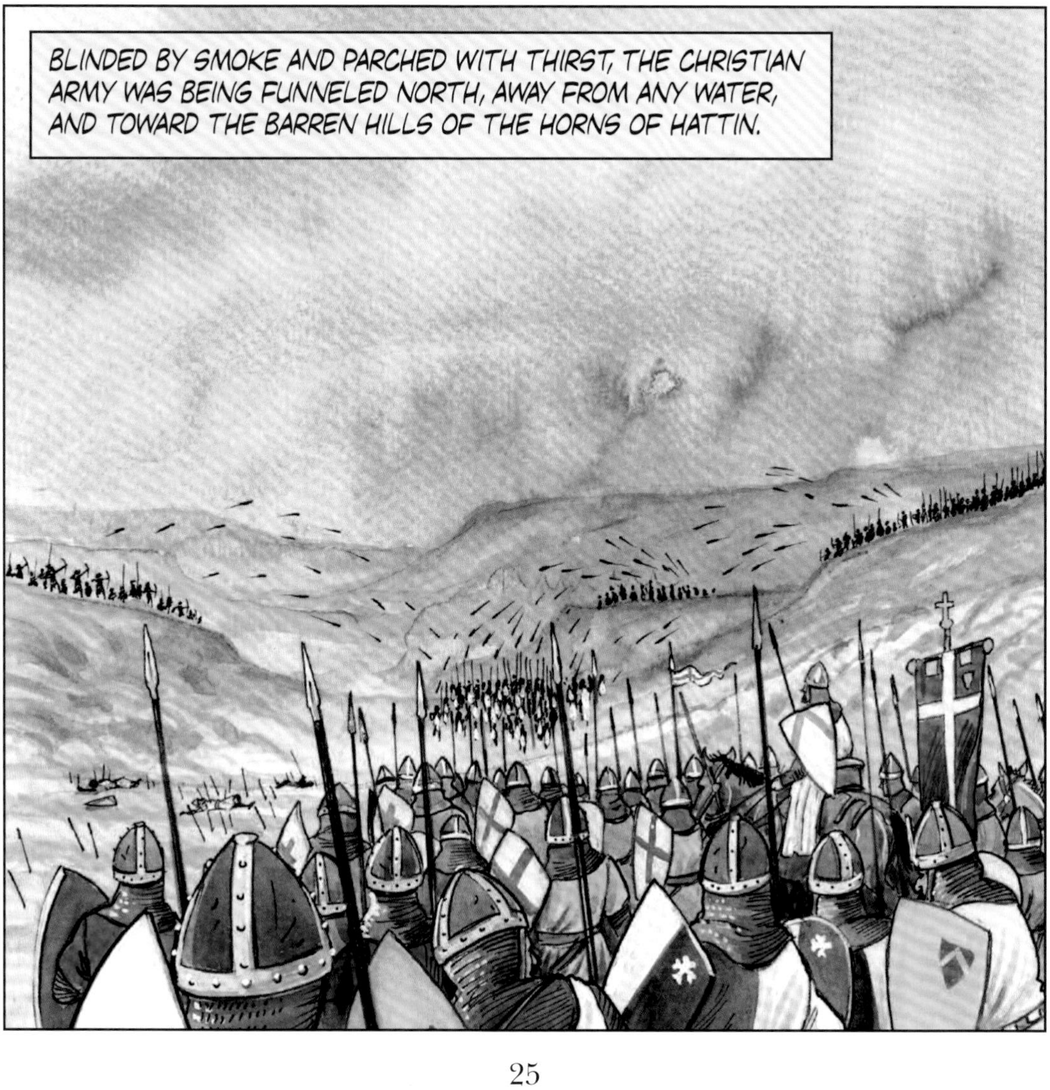
BLINDED BY SMOKE AND PARCHED WITH THIRST, THE CHRISTIAN ARMY WAS BEING FUNNELED NORTH, AWAY FROM ANY WATER, AND TOWARD THE BARREN HILLS OF THE HORNS OF HATTIN.

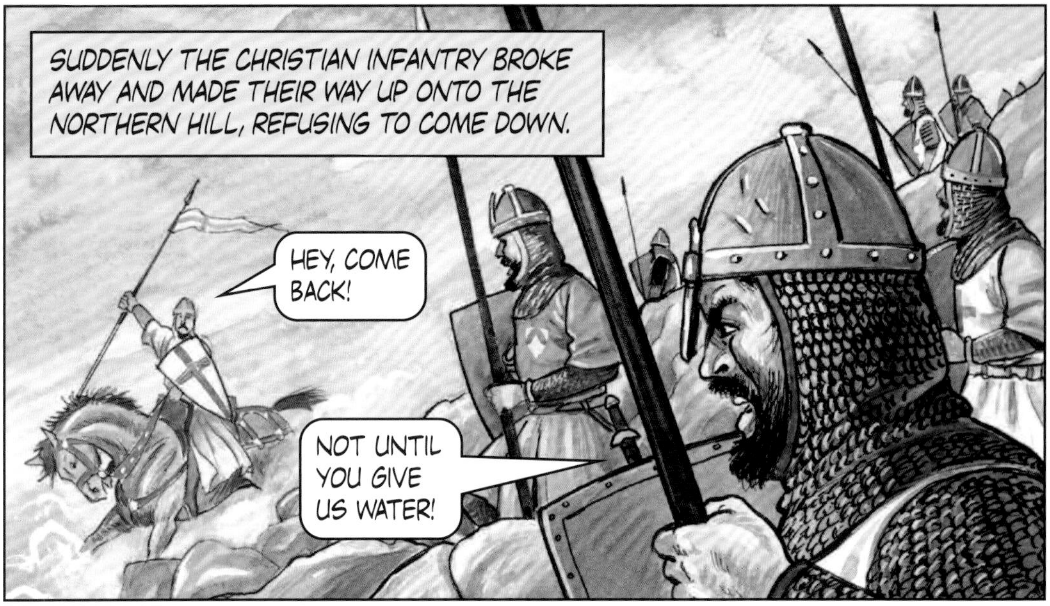
SUDDENLY THE CHRISTIAN INFANTRY BROKE AWAY AND MADE THEIR WAY UP ONTO THE NORTHERN HILL, REFUSING TO COME DOWN.
HEY, COME BACK!
NOT UNTIL YOU GIVE US WATER!

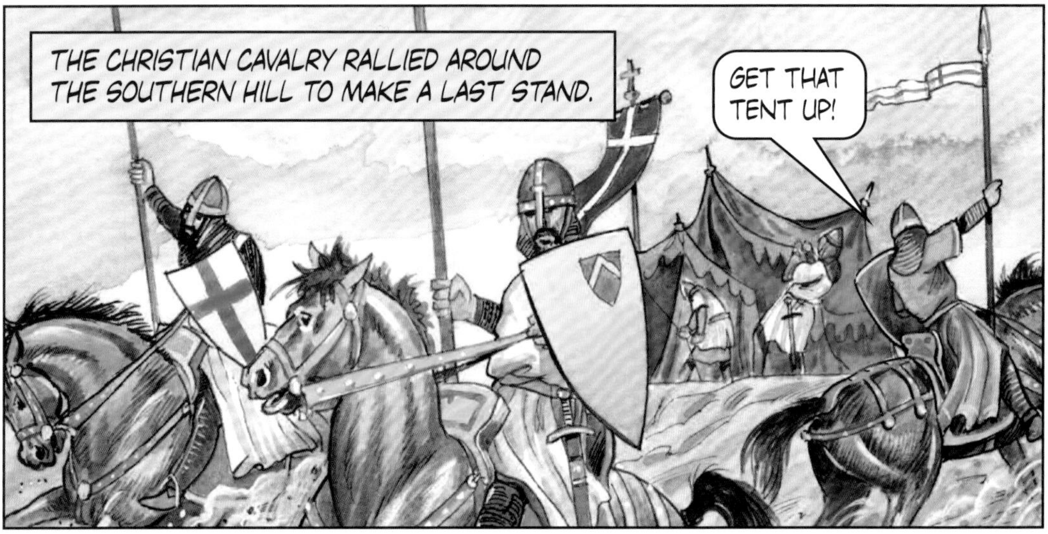
THE CHRISTIAN CAVALRY RALLIED AROUND THE SOUTHERN HILL TO MAKE A LAST STAND.
GET THAT TENT UP!

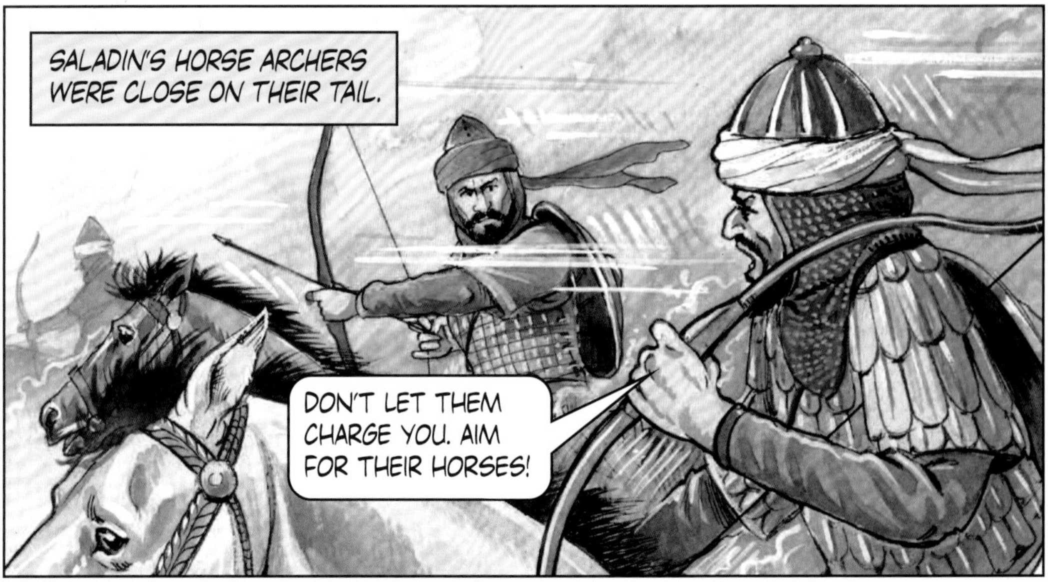
SALADIN'S HORSE ARCHERS WERE CLOSE ON THEIR TAIL.
DON'T LET THEM CHARGE YOU. AIM FOR THEIR HORSES!

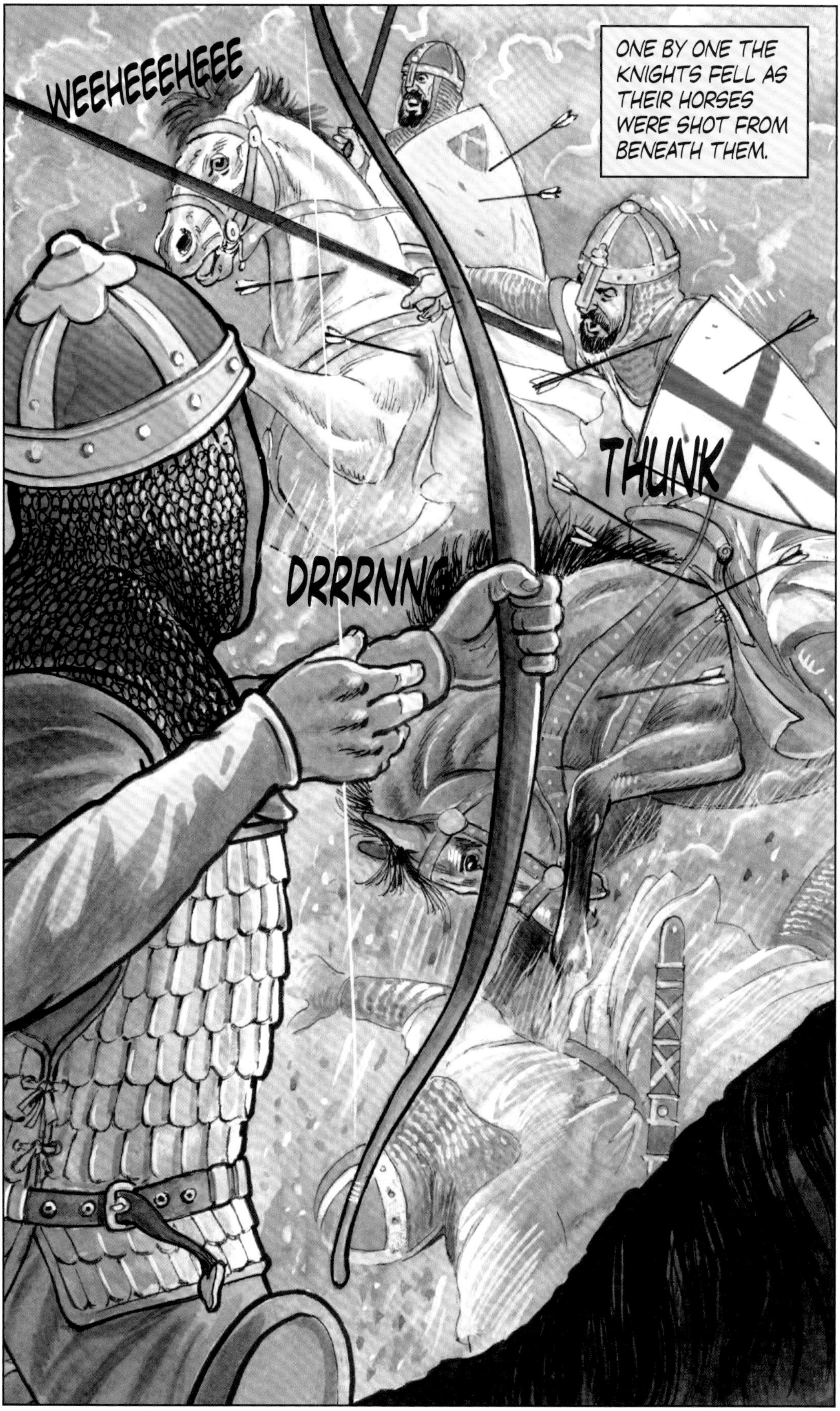
ONE BY ONE THE KNIGHTS FELL AS THEIR HORSES WERE SHOT FROM BENEATH THEM.
WEEHEEEHEEE
THUNK
DRRRNNG

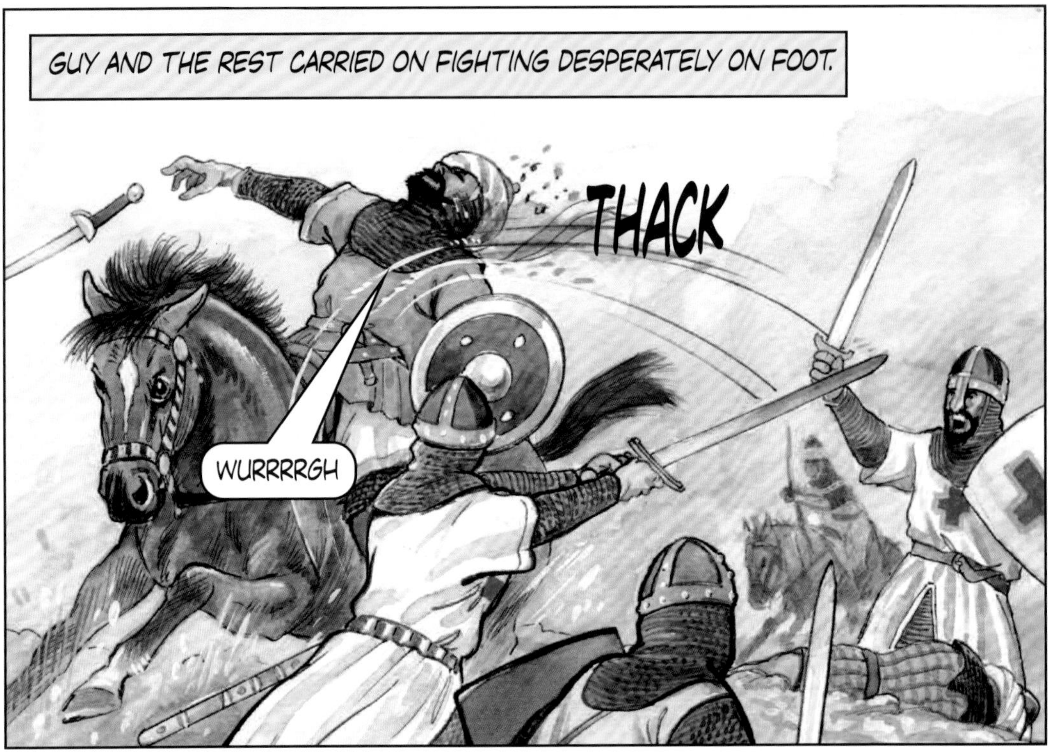
GUY AND THE REST CARRIED ON FIGHTING DESPERATELY ON FOOT.
THACK
WURRRRGH

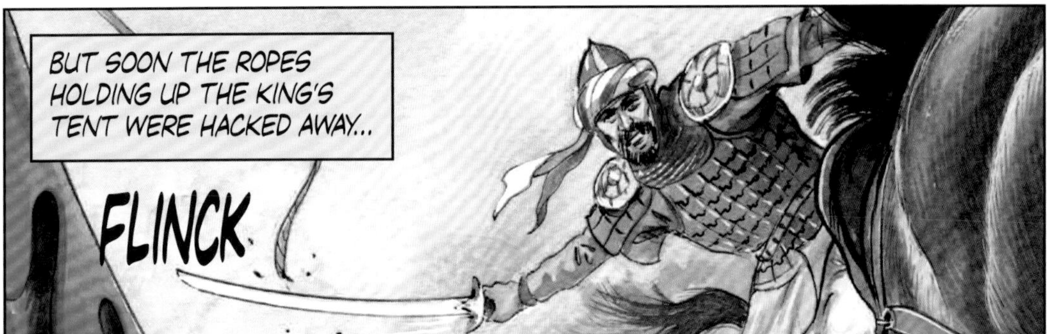
BUT SOON THE ROPES HOLDING UP THE KING'S TENT WERE HACKED AWAY...
FLINCK

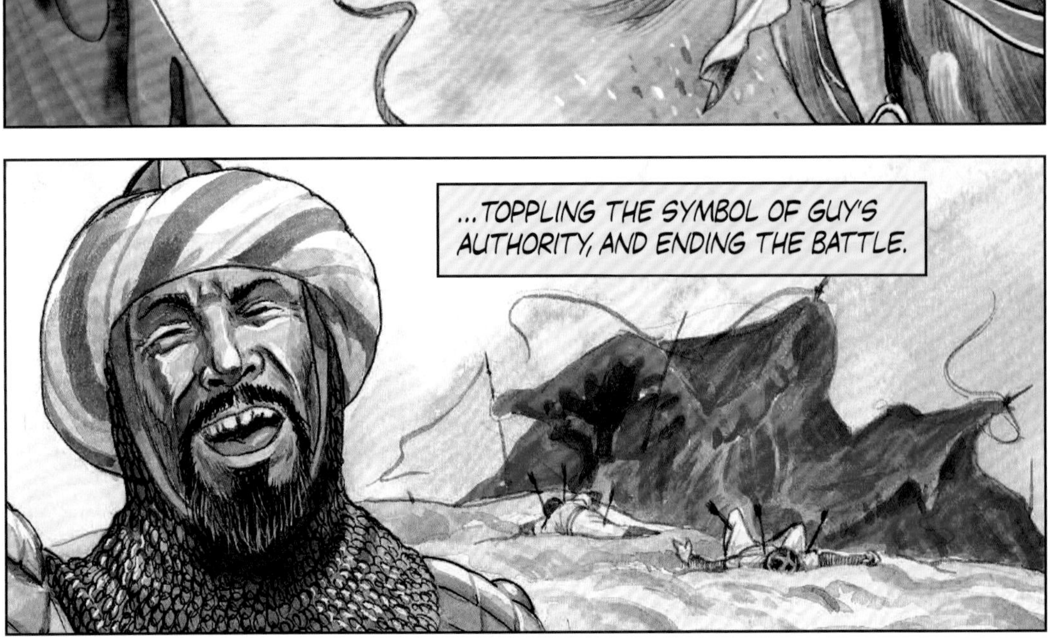
...TOPPLING THE SYMBOL OF GUY'S AUTHORITY, AND ENDING THE BATTLE.

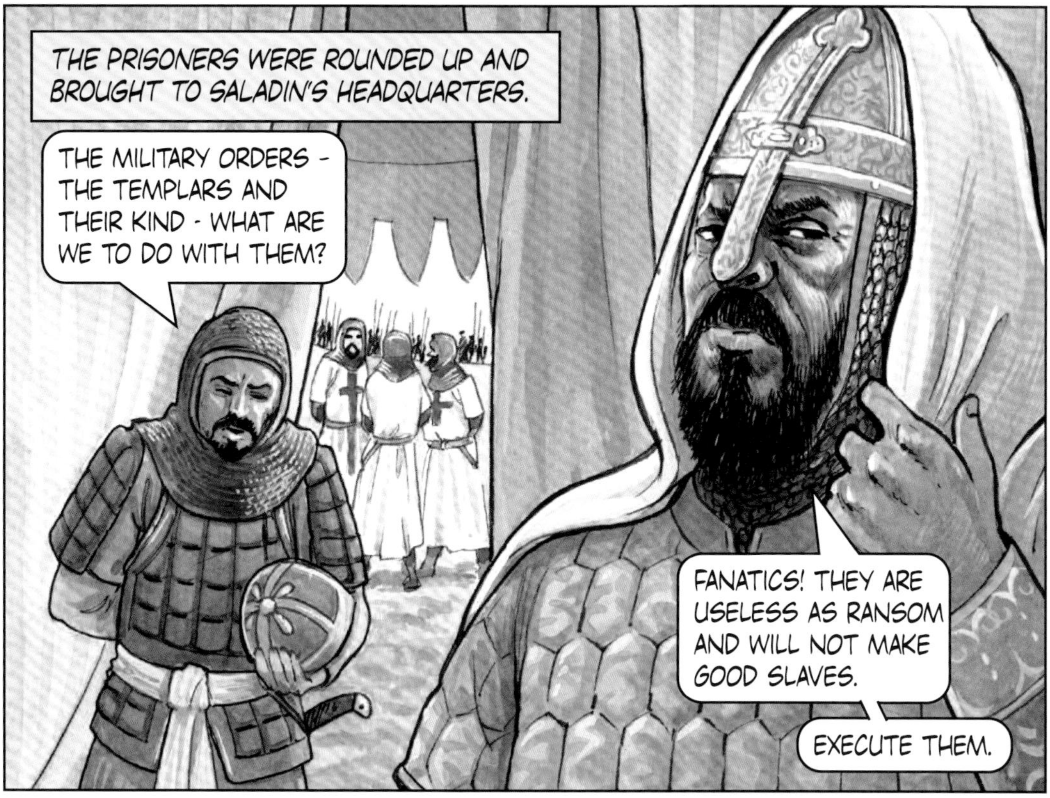
THE PRISONERS WERE ROUNDED UP AND BROUGHT TO SALADIN'S HEADQUARTERS.
THE MILITARY ORDERS - THE TEMPLARS AND THEIR KIND - WHAT ARE WE TO DO WITH THEM?
FANATICS! THEY ARE USELESS AS RANSOM AND WILL NOT MAKE GOOD SLAVES.
EXECUTE THEM.

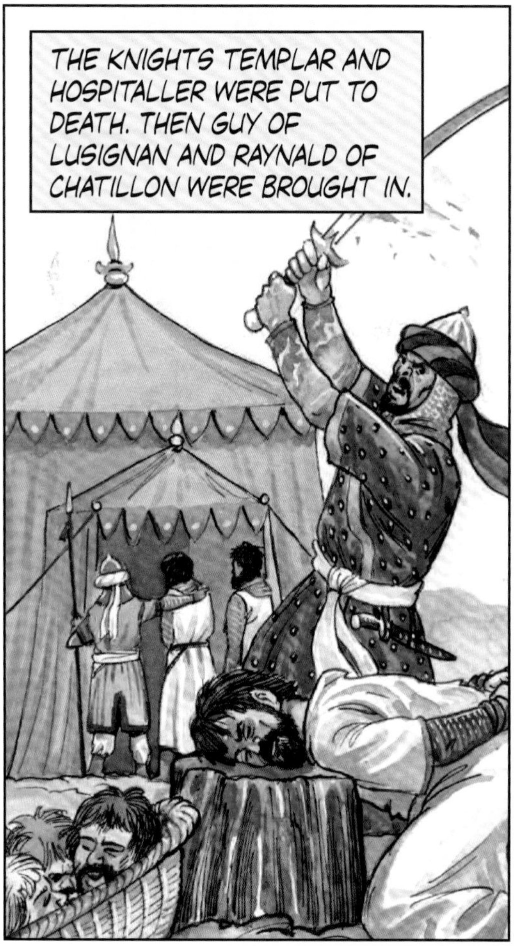
THE KNIGHTS TEMPLAR AND HOSPITALLER WERE PUT TO DEATH. THEN GUY OF LUSIGNAN AND RAYNALD OF CHATILLON WERE BROUGHT IN.

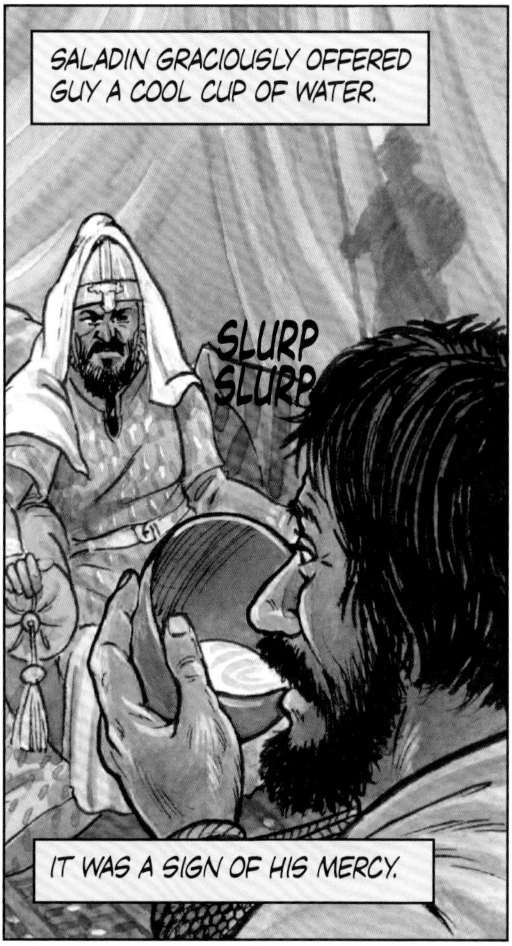
SALADIN GRACIOUSLY OFFERED GUY A COOL CUP OF WATER.
SLURP SLURP
IT WAS A SIGN OF HIS MERCY.

GUY PASSED THE CUP TO RAYNALD WHO DRANK DEEPLY, WATCHED INTENTLY BY SALADIN.

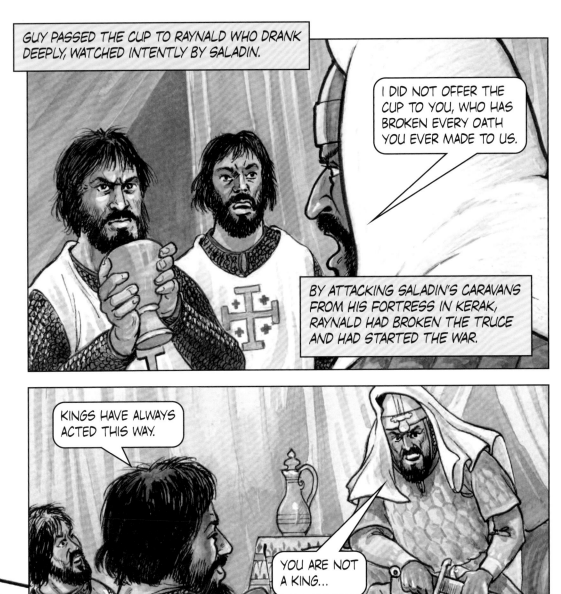

I DID NOT OFFER THE CUP TO YOU, WHO HAS BROKEN EVERY OATH YOU EVER MADE TO US.

BY ATTACKING SALADIN'S CARAVANS FROM HIS FORTRESS IN KERAK, RAYNALD HAD BROKEN THE TRUCE AND HAD STARTED THE WAR.

KINGS HAVE ALWAYS ACTED THIS WAY.

YOU ARE NOT A KING...

...AND I AM NOT BOUND BY RULES OF HOSPITALITY...

WITH ONE SWIFT STROKE SALADIN REMOVED HIS HEAD.

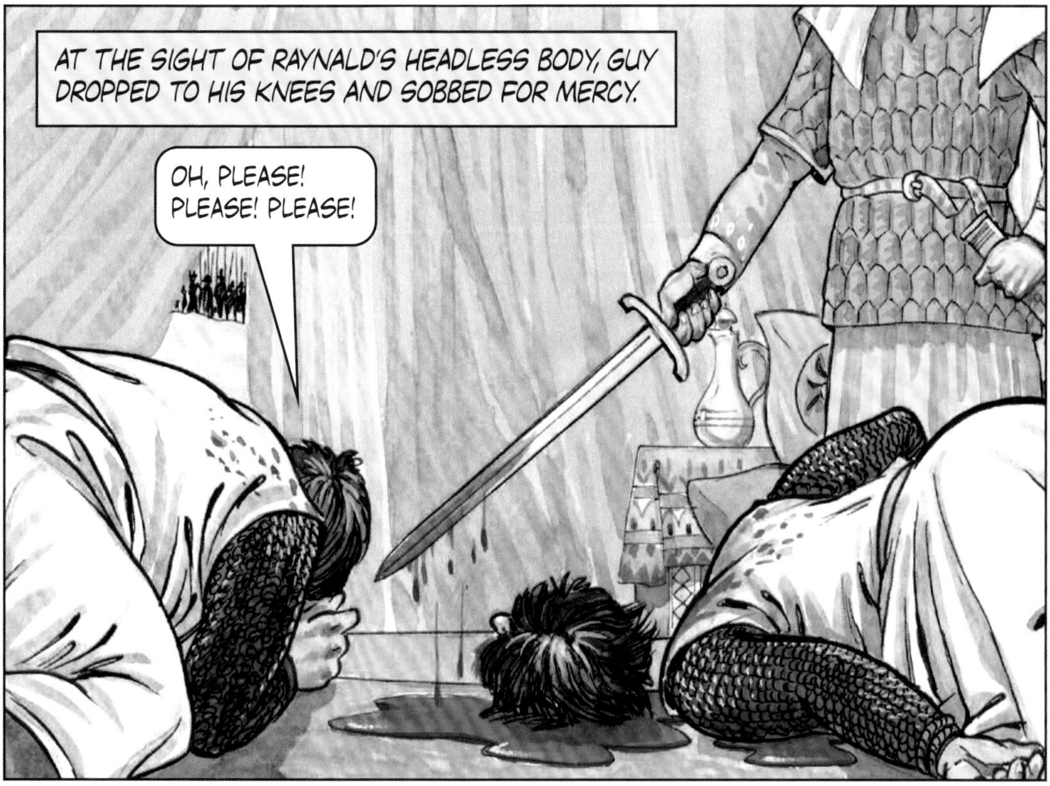
AT THE SIGHT OF RAYNALD'S HEADLESS BODY, GUY DROPPED TO HIS KNEES AND SOBBED FOR MERCY.
OH, PLEASE! PLEASE! PLEASE!

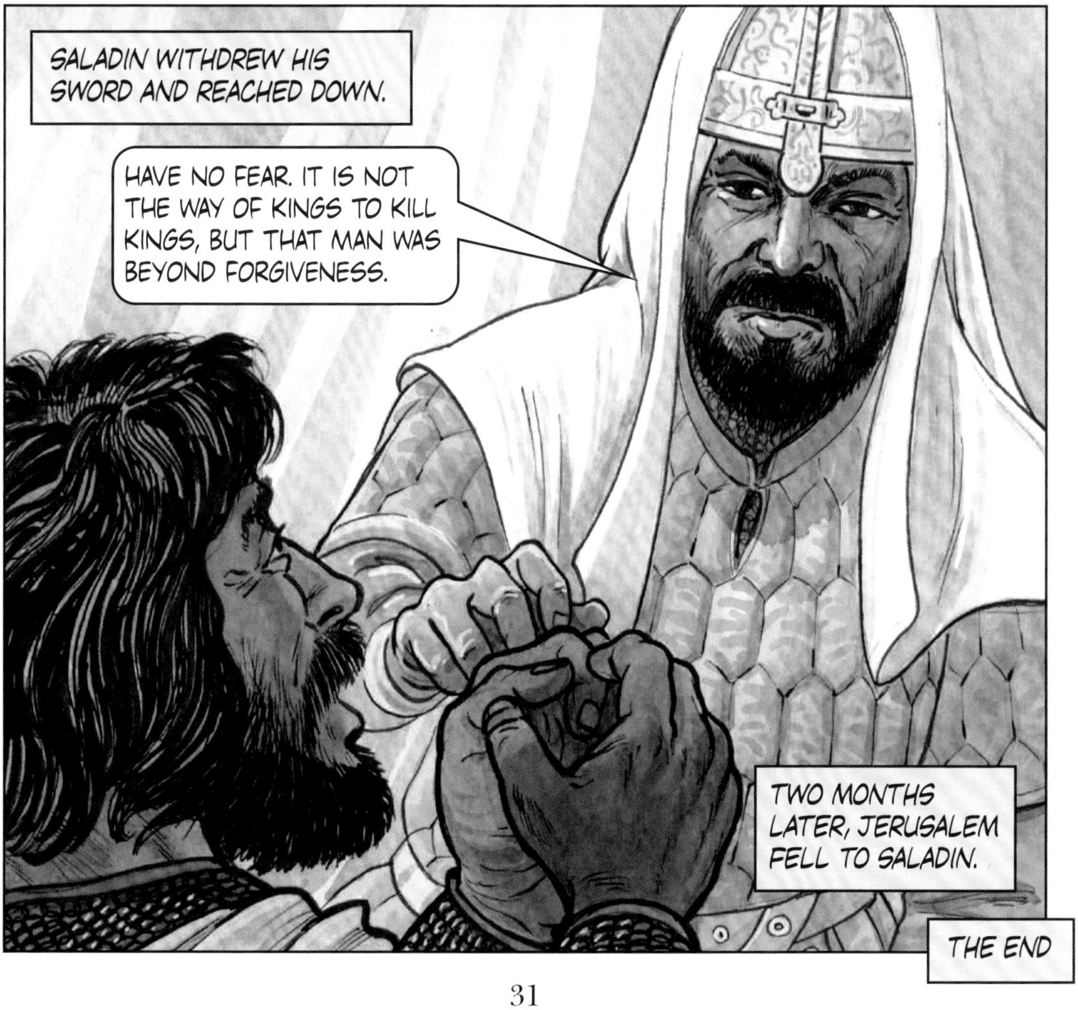
SALADIN WITHDREW HIS SWORD AND REACHED DOWN.
HAVE NO FEAR. IT IS NOT THE WAY OF KINGS TO KILL KINGS, BUT THAT MAN WAS BEYOND FORGIVENESS.
TWO MONTHS LATER, JERUSALEM FELL TO SALADIN.
THE END

The Defense of Jaffa
The Third Crusade

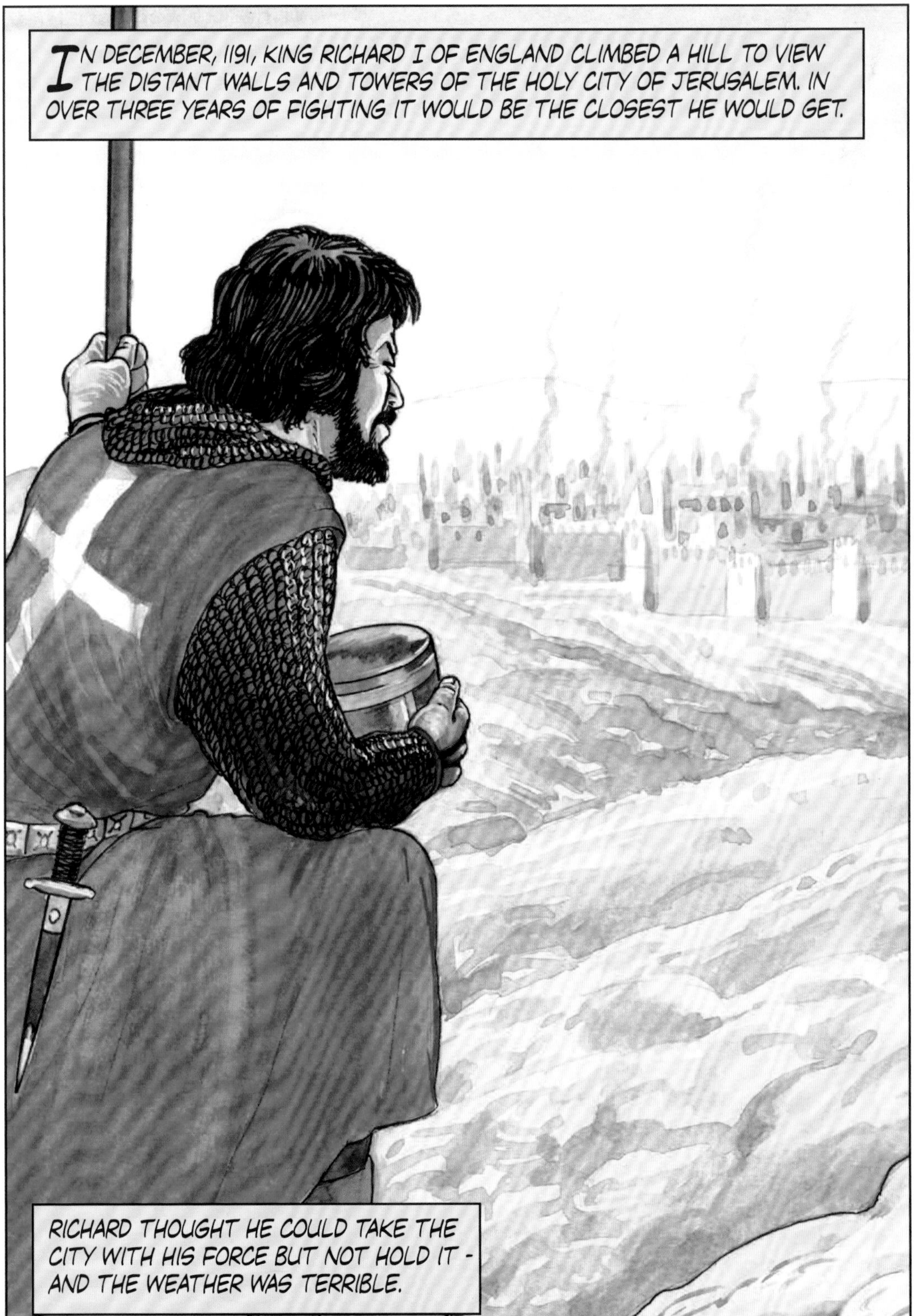
IN DECEMBER, 1191, KING RICHARD I OF ENGLAND CLIMBED A HILL TO VIEW THE DISTANT WALLS AND TOWERS OF THE HOLY CITY OF JERUSALEM. IN OVER THREE YEARS OF FIGHTING IT WOULD BE THE CLOSEST HE WOULD GET.
RICHARD THOUGHT HE COULD TAKE THE CITY WITH HIS FORCE BUT NOT HOLD IT - AND THE WEATHER WAS TERRIBLE.

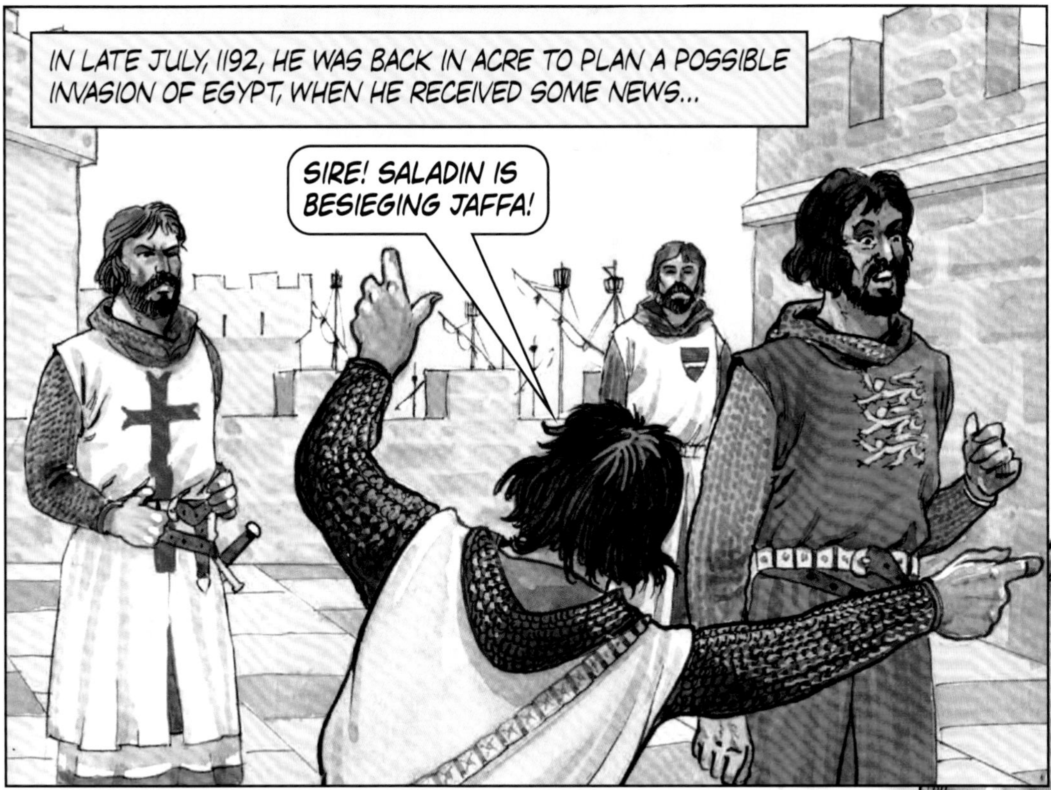
IN LATE JULY, 1192, HE WAS BACK IN ACRE TO PLAN A POSSIBLE INVASION OF EGYPT, WHEN HE RECEIVED SOME NEWS...
SIRE! SALADIN IS BESIEGING JAFFA!

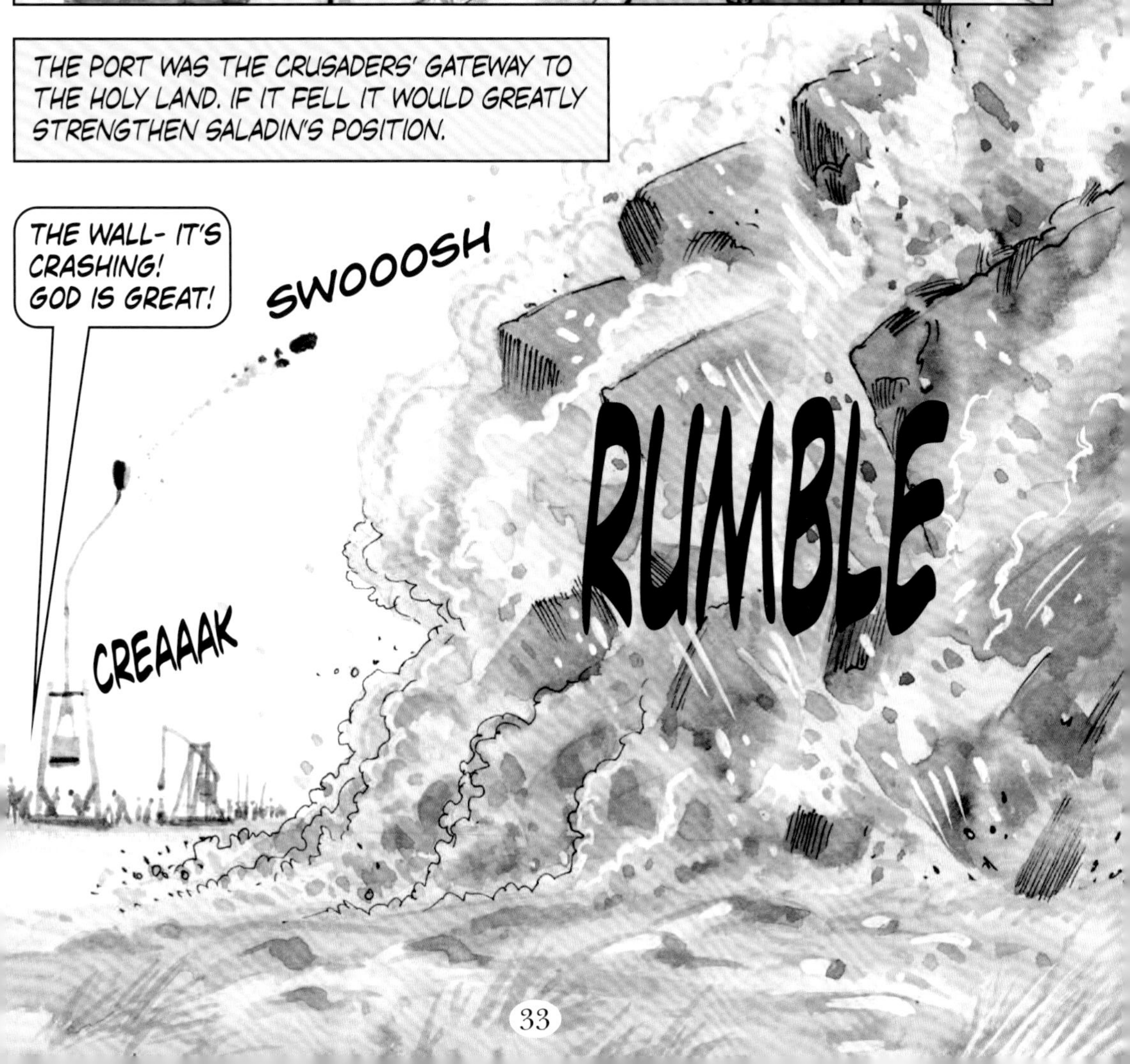
THE PORT WAS THE CRUSADERS' GATEWAY TO THE HOLY LAND. IF IT FELL IT WOULD GREATLY STRENGTHEN SALADIN'S POSITION.
THE WALL- IT'S CRASHING! GOD IS GREAT!
SWOOOSH
RUMBLE
CREAAAK

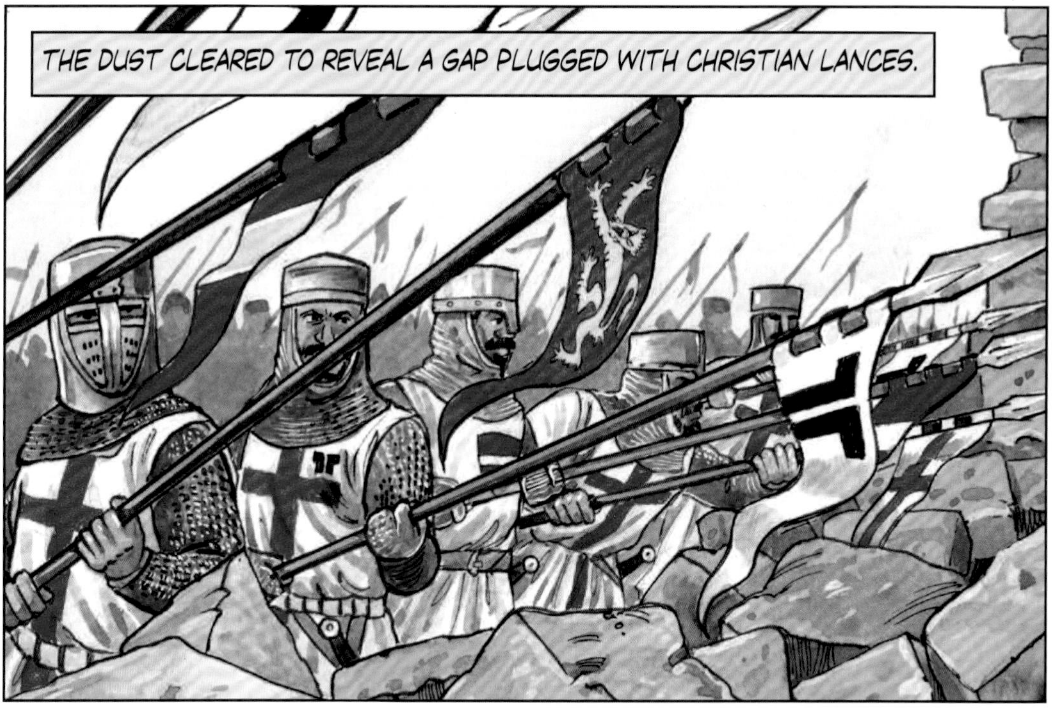
THE DUST CLEARED TO REVEAL A GAP PLUGGED WITH CHRISTIAN LANCES.

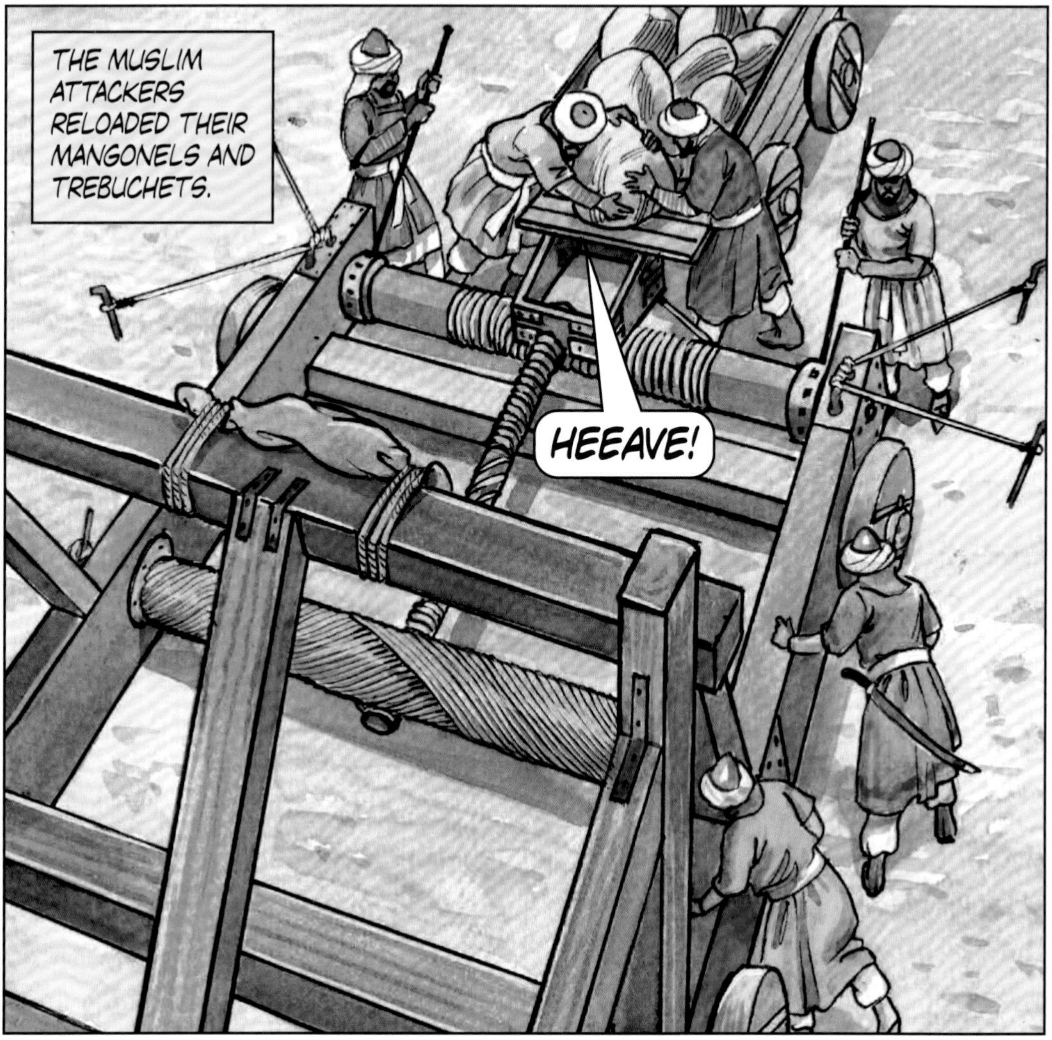
THE MUSLIM ATTACKERS RELOADED THEIR MANGONELS AND TREBUCHETS.
HEEAVE!

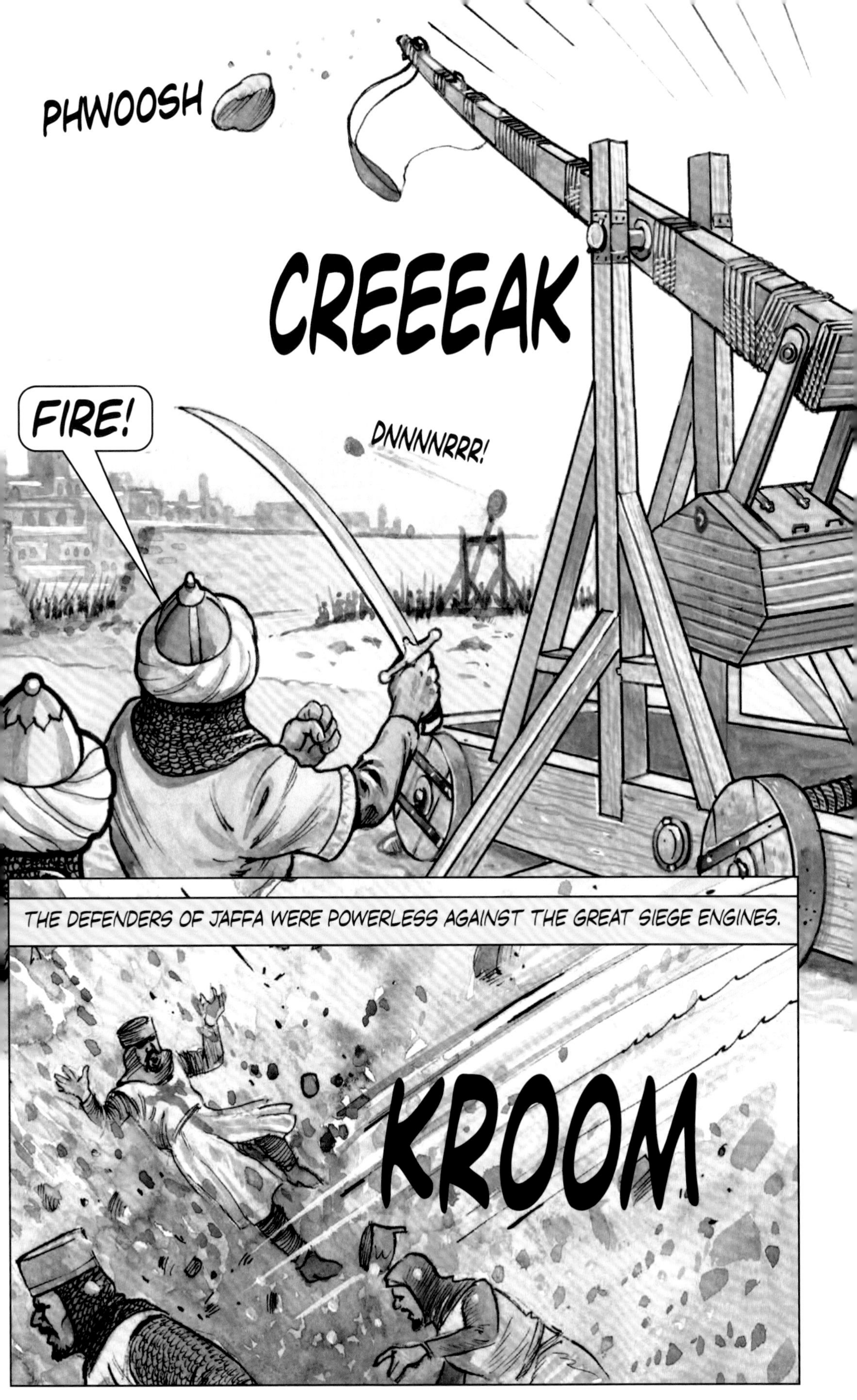
PHWOOSH
CREEEAK
FIRE!
DNNNNRRR!
THE DEFENDERS OF JAFFA WERE POWERLESS AGAINST THE GREAT SIEGE ENGINES.
KROOM

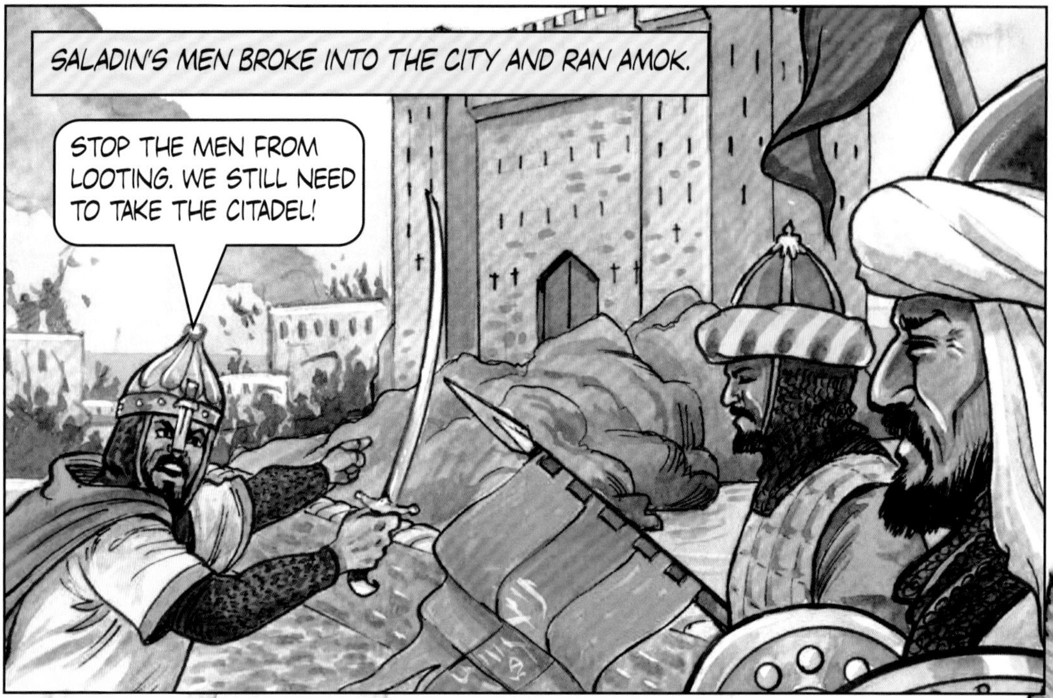
SALADIN'S MEN BROKE INTO THE CITY AND RAN AMOK.
STOP THE MEN FROM LOOTING. WE STILL NEED TO TAKE THE CITADEL!

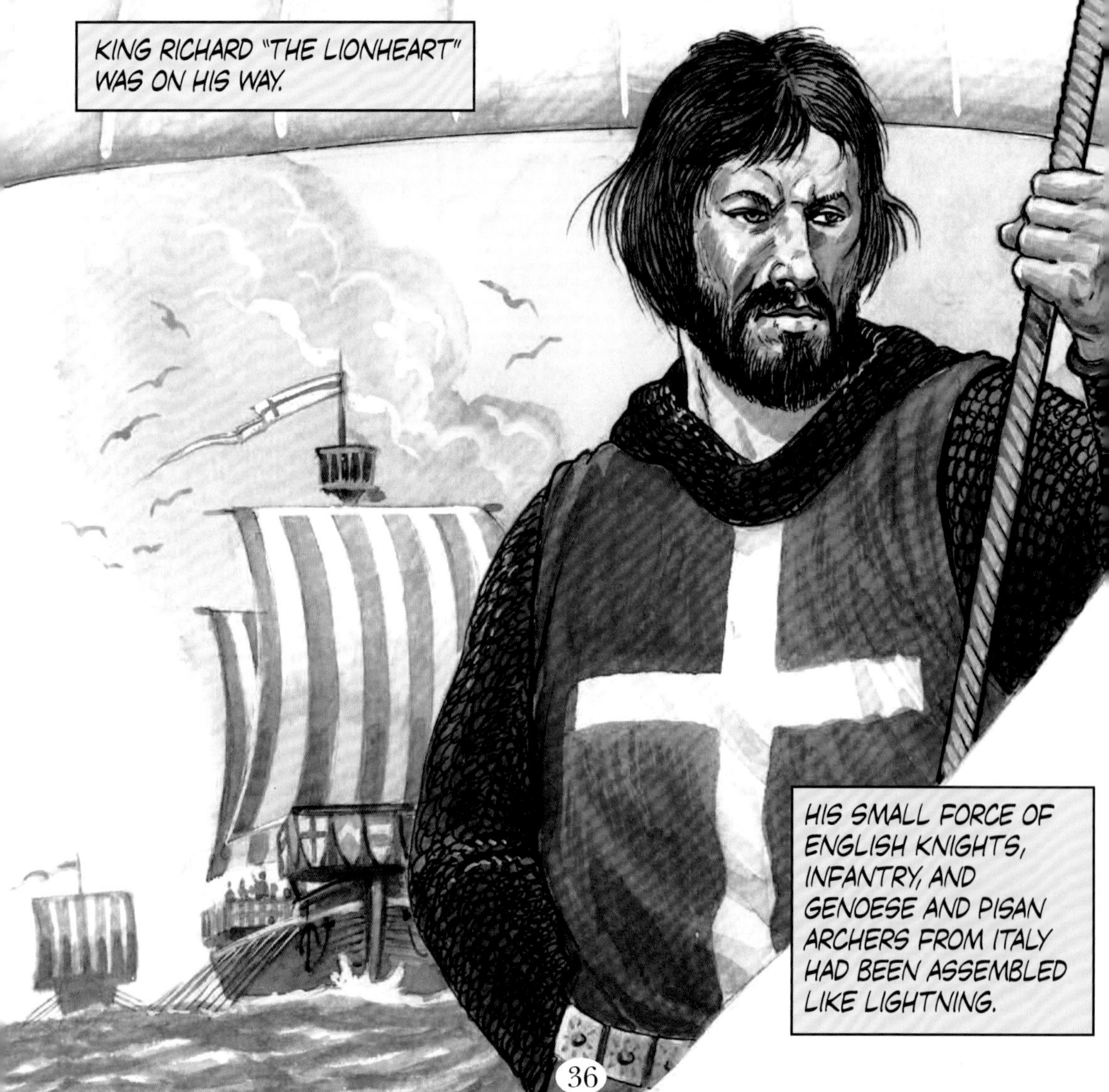
KING RICHARD "THE LIONHEART" WAS ON HIS WAY.
HIS SMALL FORCE OF ENGLISH KNIGHTS, INFANTRY, AND GENOESE AND PISAN ARCHERS FROM ITALY HAD BEEN ASSEMBLED LIKE LIGHTNING.

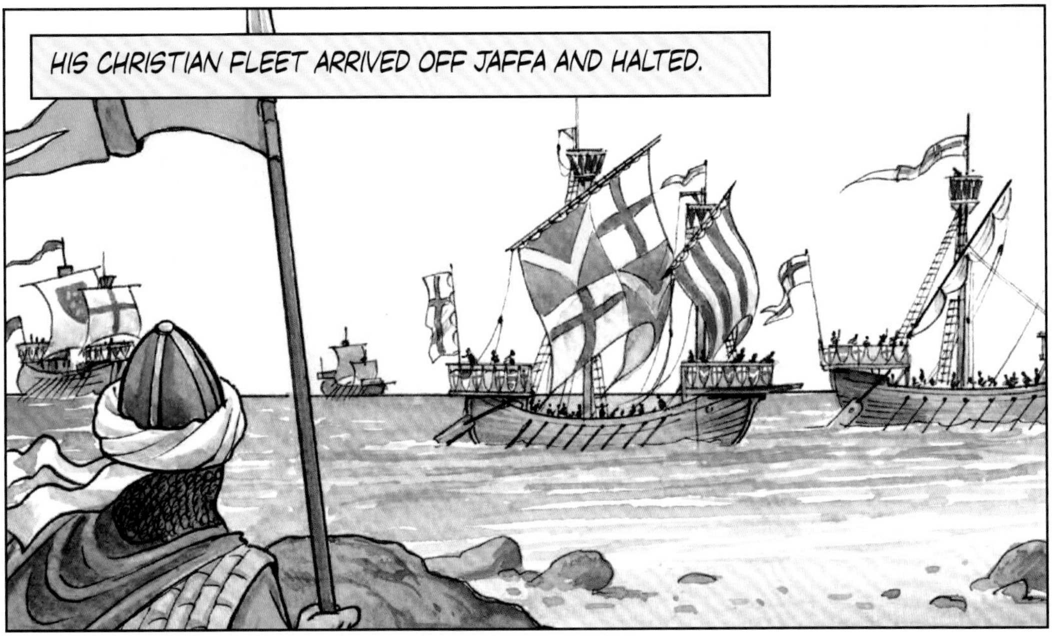
HIS CHRISTIAN FLEET ARRIVED OFF JAFFA AND HALTED.

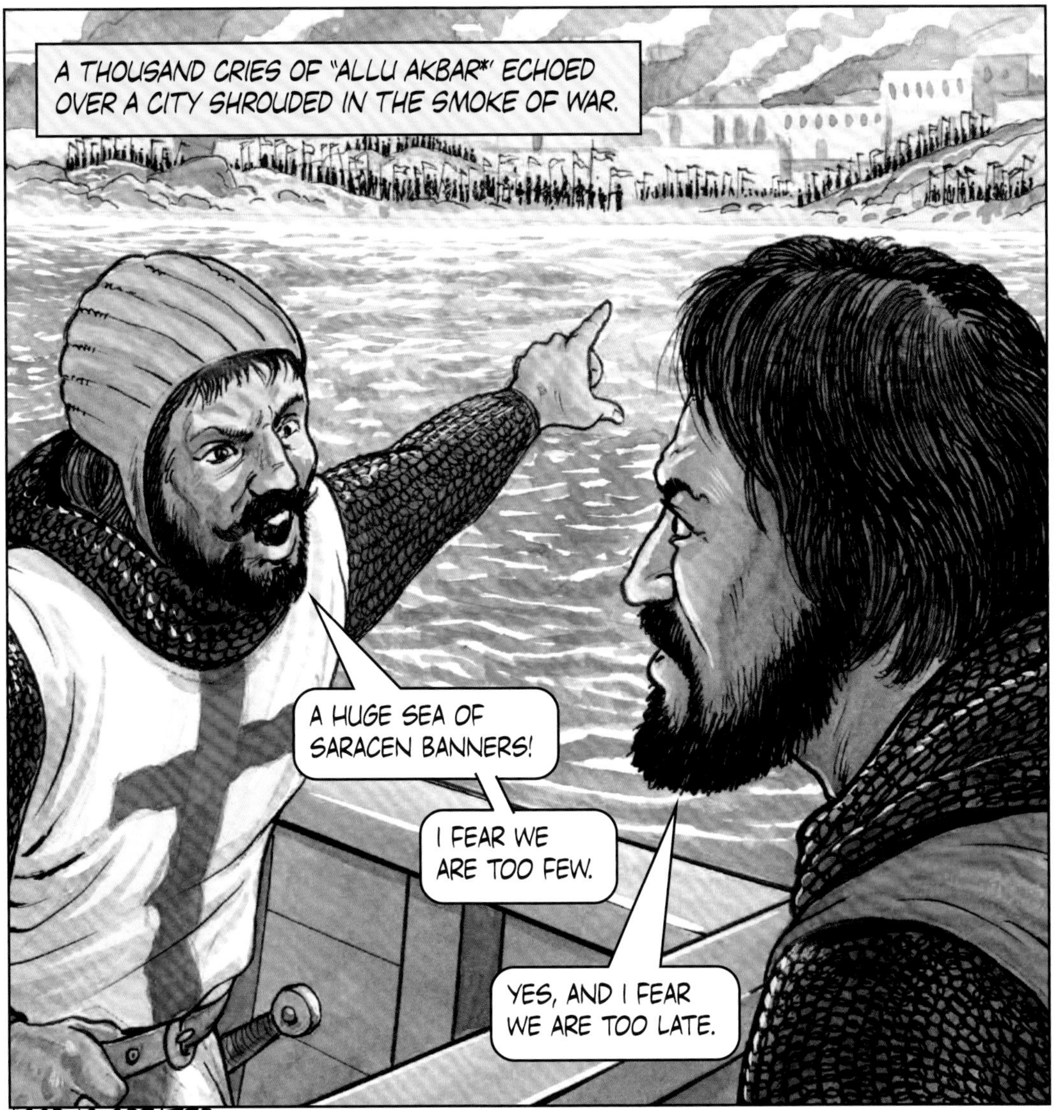
A THOUSAND CRIES OF "ALLU AKBAR*" ECHOED OVER A CITY SHROUDED IN THE SMOKE OF WAR.
A HUGE SEA OF SARACEN BANNERS!
I FEAR WE ARE TOO FEW.
YES, AND I FEAR WE ARE TOO LATE.

*GOD IS GREATER

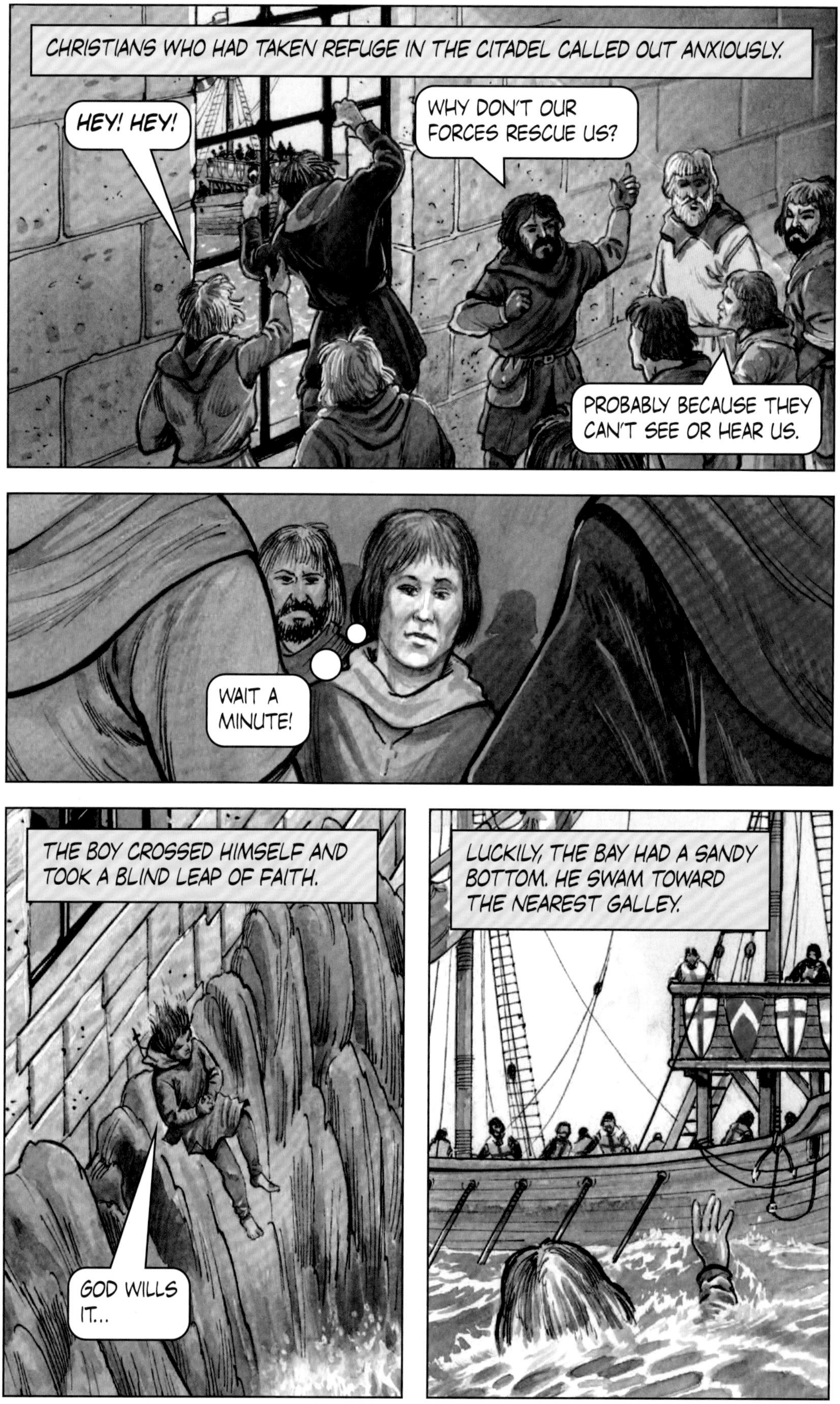

CHRISTIANS WHO HAD TAKEN REFUGE IN THE CITADEL CALLED OUT ANXIOUSLY.
HEY! HEY!
WHY DON'T OUR FORCES RESCUE US?
PROBABLY BECAUSE THEY CAN'T SEE OR HEAR US.
WAIT A MINUTE!
THE BOY CROSSED HIMSELF AND TOOK A BLIND LEAP OF FAITH.
GOD WILLS IT...
LUCKILY, THE BAY HAD A SANDY BOTTOM. HE SWAM TOWARD THE NEAREST GALLEY.

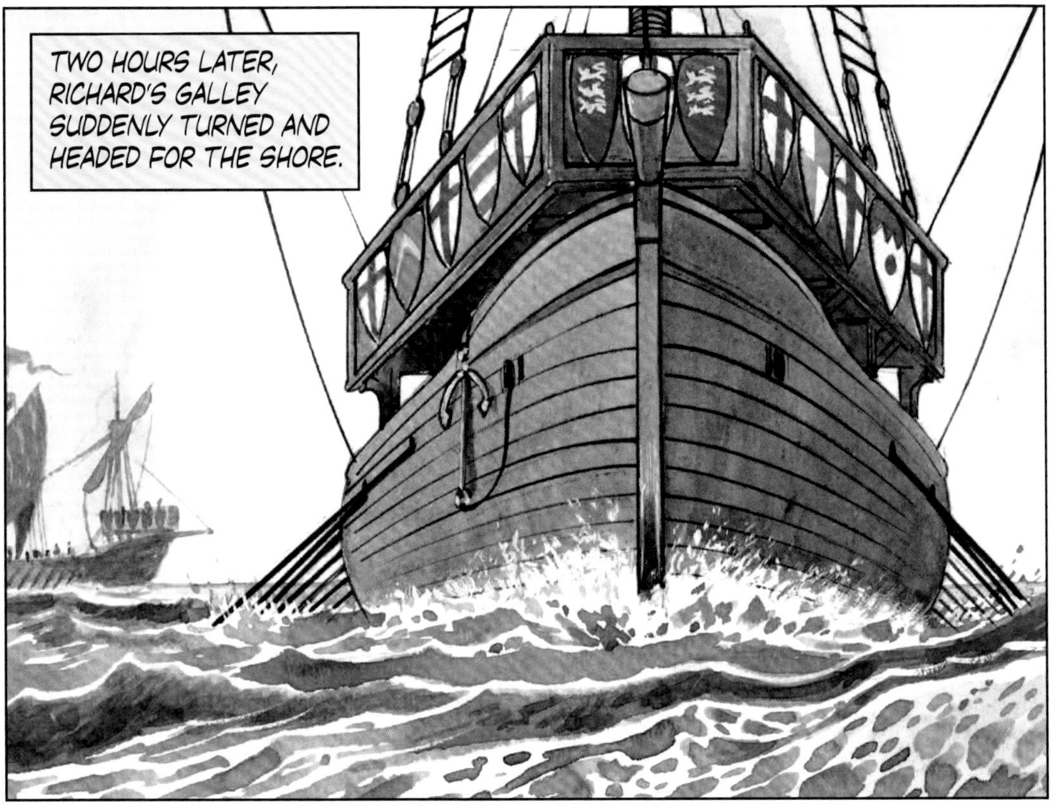
TWO HOURS LATER, RICHARD'S GALLEY SUDDENLY TURNED AND HEADED FOR THE SHORE.

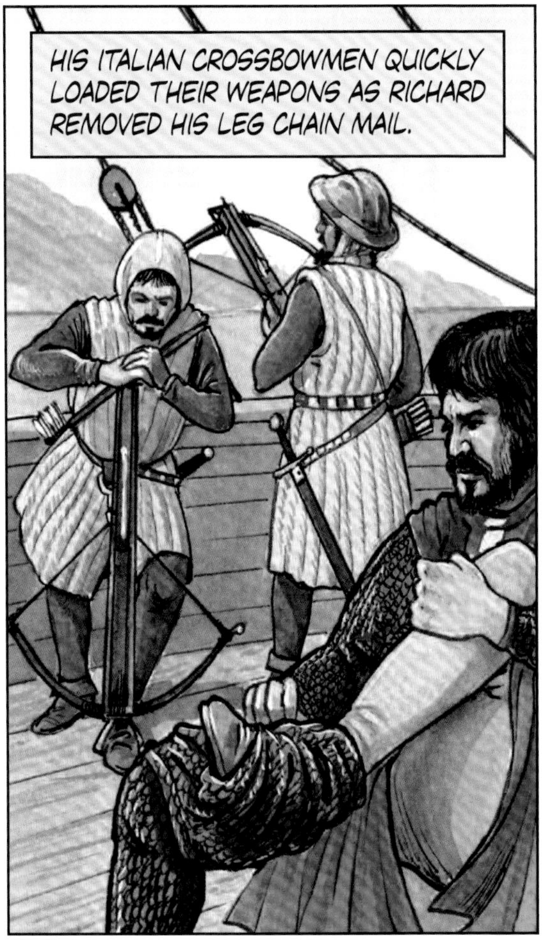
HIS ITALIAN CROSSBOWMEN QUICKLY LOADED THEIR WEAPONS AS RICHARD REMOVED HIS LEG CHAIN MAIL.

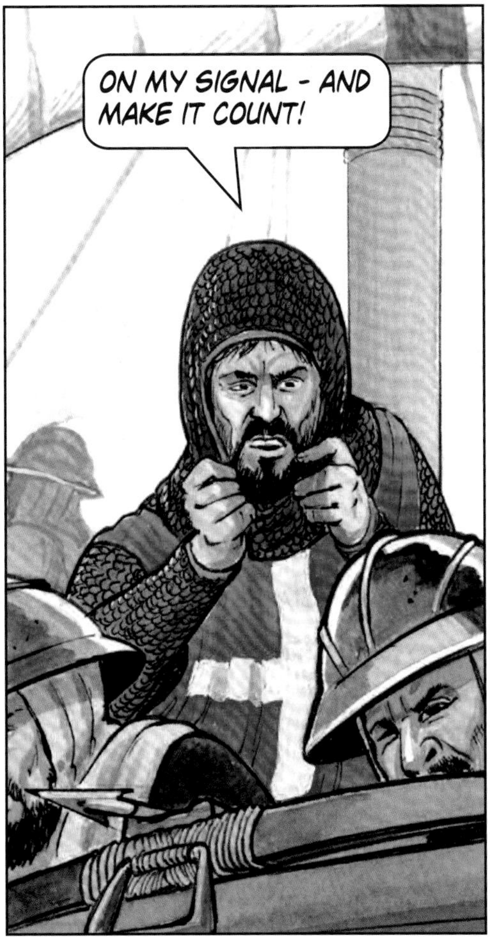
ON MY SIGNAL - AND MAKE IT COUNT!

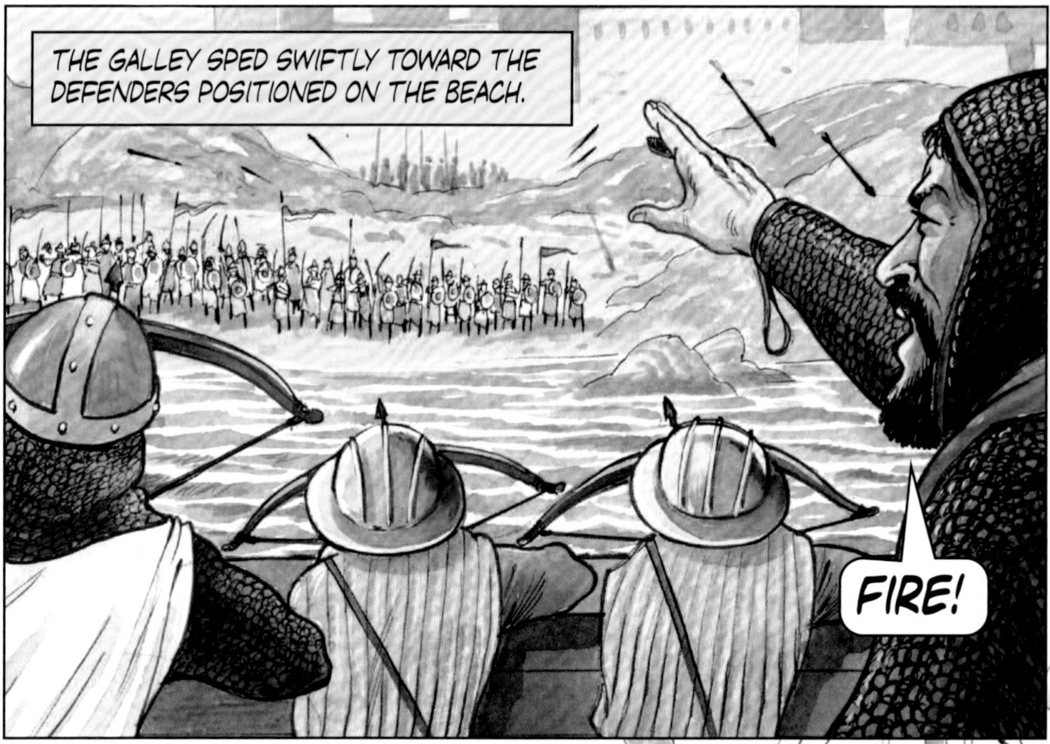
THE GALLEY SPED SWIFTLY TOWARD THE DEFENDERS POSITIONED ON THE BEACH.
FIRE!

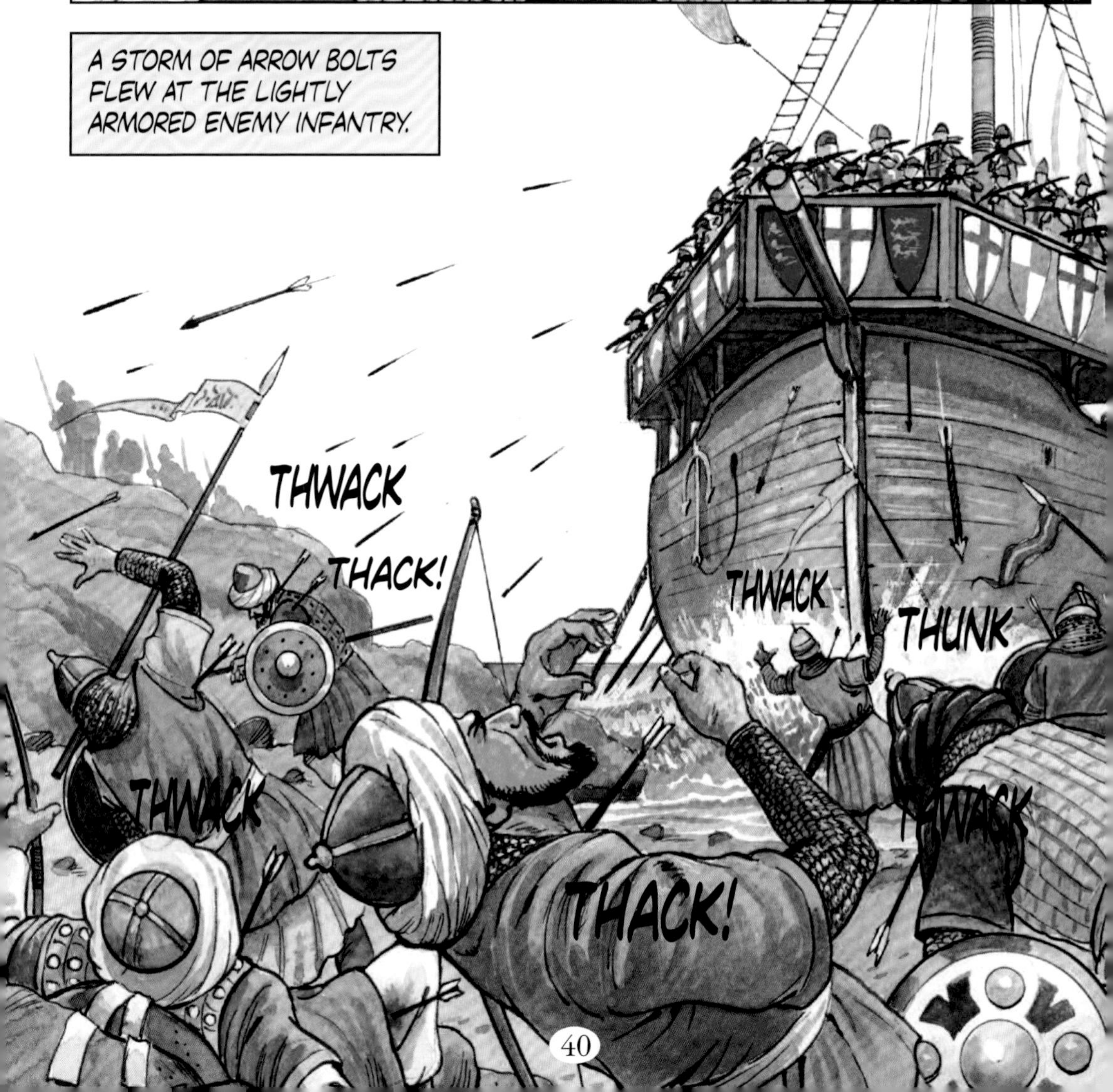
A STORM OF ARROW BOLTS FLEW AT THE LIGHTLY ARMORED ENEMY INFANTRY.
THWACK
THACK!
THWACK
THUNK
THWACK
THWACK
THACK!

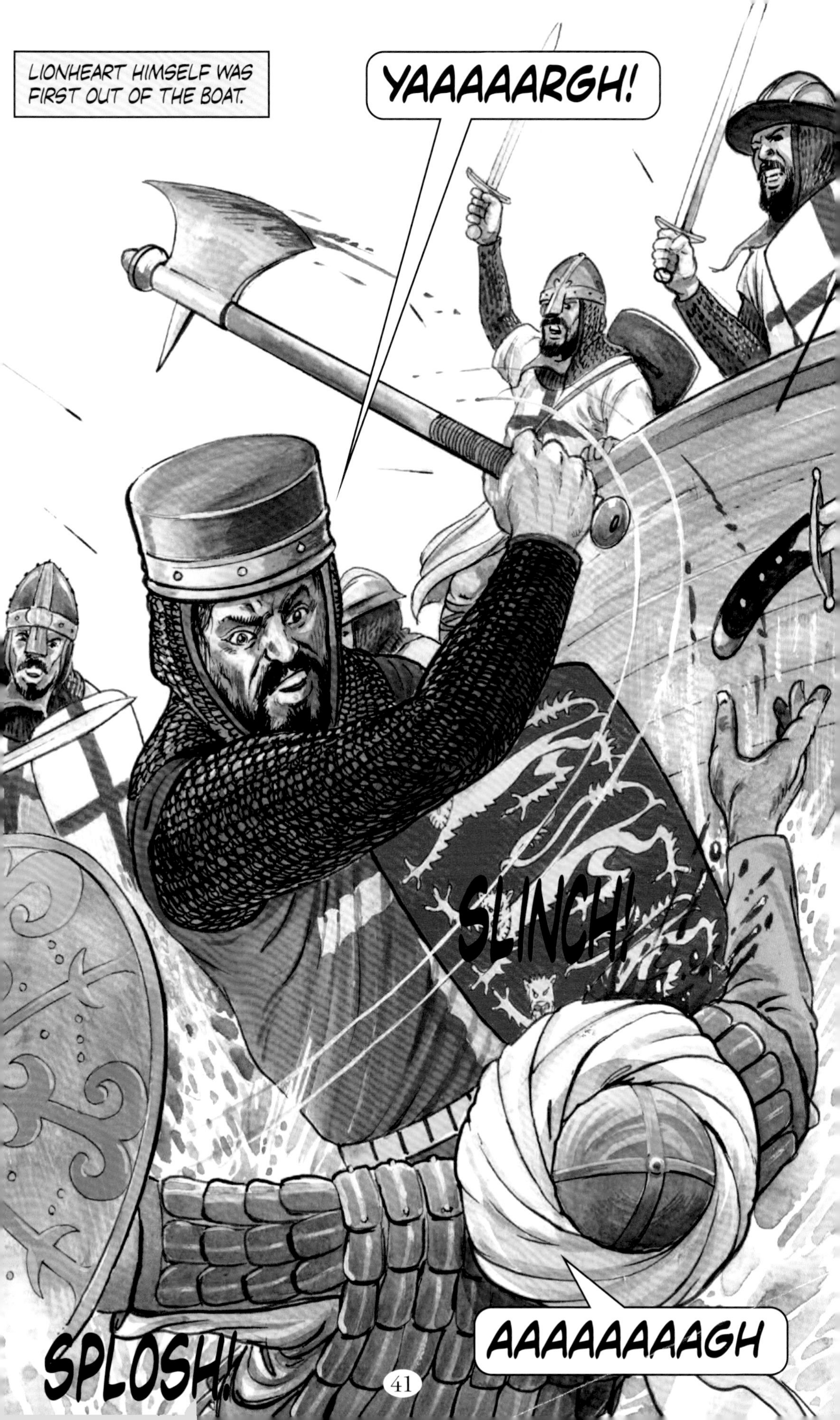
LIONHEART HIMSELF WAS FIRST OUT OF THE BOAT.
YAAAAARGH!
SLINCH!
AAAAAAAAGH
SPLOSH!

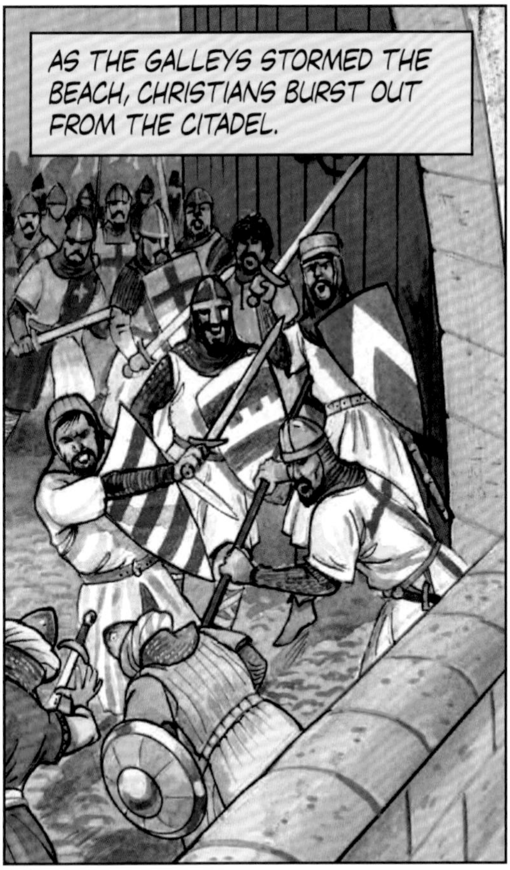
AS THE GALLEYS STORMED THE BEACH, CHRISTIANS BURST OUT FROM THE CITADEL.

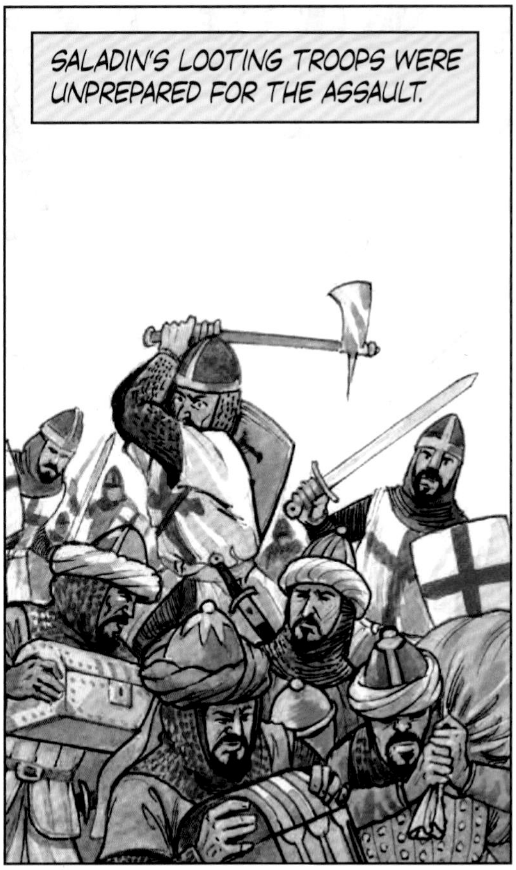
SALADIN'S LOOTING TROOPS WERE UNPREPARED FOR THE ASSAULT.

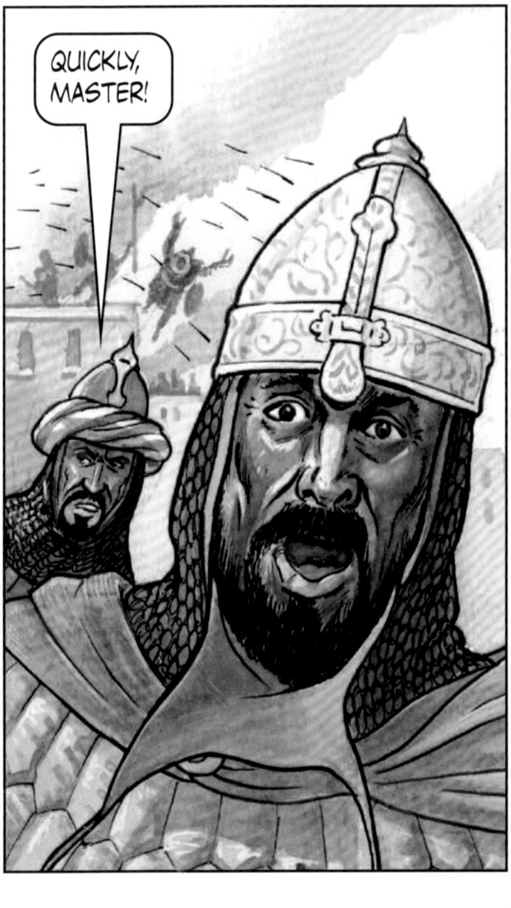
QUICKLY, MASTER!

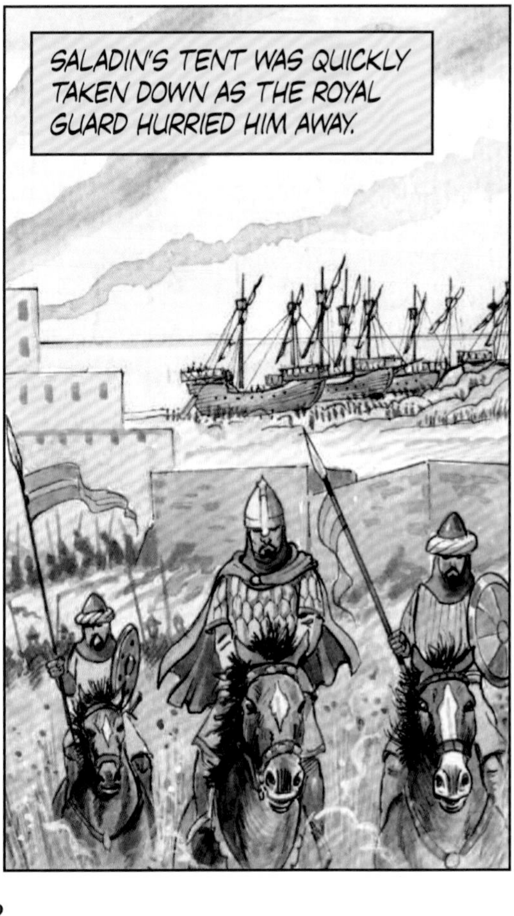
SALADIN'S TENT WAS QUICKLY TAKEN DOWN AS THE ROYAL GUARD HURRIED HIM AWAY.

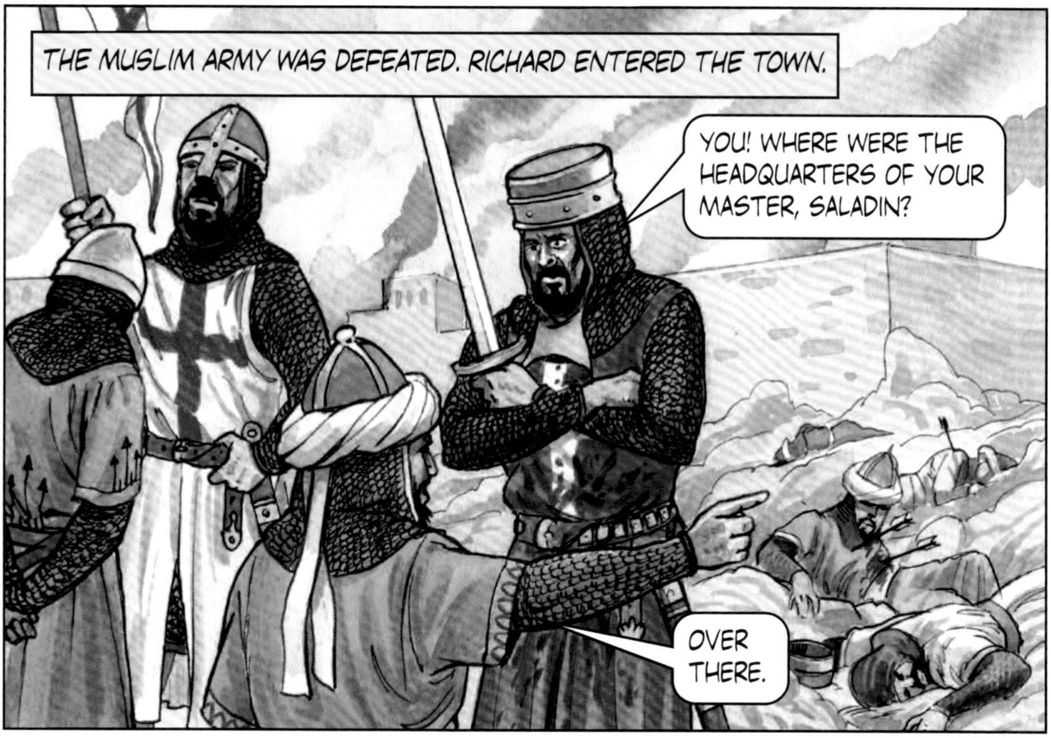
THE MUSLIM ARMY WAS DEFEATED. RICHARD ENTERED THE TOWN.
YOU! WHERE WERE THE HEADQUARTERS OF YOUR MASTER, SALADIN?
OVER THERE.

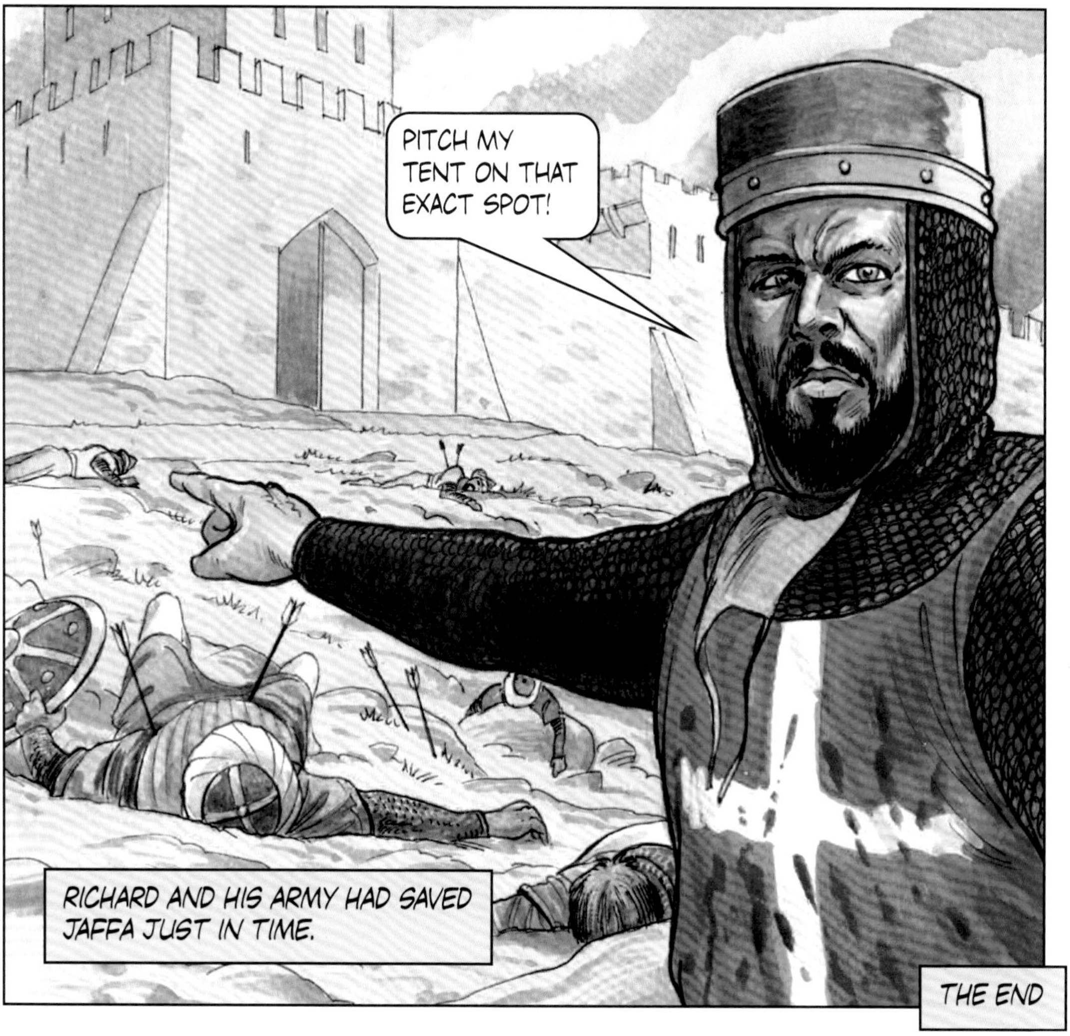
PITCH MY TENT ON THAT EXACT SPOT!
RICHARD AND HIS ARMY HAD SAVED JAFFA JUST IN TIME.
THE END

Diminishing Returns

Before he left Acre, Richard had sent a force overland to Jaffa to reinforce his position. They were slow in arriving so he camped outside the city and prepared his tiny force for the expected counterattack…

Richard I bids farewell to the Holy Land.

LIONHEART

Sure enough, wave after wave of enraged horse-mounted archers battled the thin line of crusaders, but Richard's force held out until the attack was exhausted. He had beaten Saladin at every military engagement, but Richard, who had been troubled by sickness all through the campaign, suddenly got very sick indeed.

In a show of respect between kings, Saladin had fresh fruits and ice delivered to Richard's bedside and the two enemies began peace talks. Richard was willing to exchange Ascalon (an Egyptian fortress) for money, and to leave Jerusalem alone if the crusader states could be reestablished along the coast.

Saladin agreed and also granted pilgrims the right to visit Jerusalem. Richard's military expertise had won back at least some of Outremer.

THE FOURTH CRUSADE

A truce remained over the Holy Land so the Fourth Crusade, in 1202, was to be directed at the heart of the Ayyubid Empire in Cairo, Egypt. But when the crusaders arrived at Constantinople in Byzantium, in the eastern Christian empire, they sacked it instead. The Pope was furious but powerless to stop them.

Pope Innocent III was the last pope to authorize a big crusade.

THE FIFTH CRUSADE

In 1213, the Pope again called for a crusade and, four years later, the largest royal army in crusader history, led by King Andrew II of Hungary, landed in the Holy Land

Damietta was a key Egyptian port.

to take Jerusalem. The Muslims in the city destroyed its walls and fled, but the campaign gradually faded. The next year a new European army arrived and conquered Damietta, but their march on Cairo was thwarted by weather and Ayyubid troops.

THE SIXTH CRUSADE

In the first crusade not declared by a pope, Holy Roman Emperor Frederick II invaded the Holy Land with a small force and successfully negotiated for the possession of Jerusalem on the condition that its walls were not rebuilt. This agreement, won without bloodshed, lasted for 11 years.

Frederick II negotiates with al-Kamil, sultan of Egypt.

THE SEVENTH CRUSADE

In 1244, Khwarezian Turks, forced east by the Mongols, invaded the eastern Mediterranean and took over Jerusalem. A four-year crusade, led by French king Louis IX against Egypt, ended with his army's defeat and his own capture and ransom.

THE EIGHT AND NINTH CRUSADES

Louis returned in 1271 but died in Tunisia while preparing to invade Egypt. Charles I of Sicily took over and, with Prince Edward of

England, sailed to Acre to defend the remaining crusader states against the Mamluk Turks who now controlled the area.

This ninth and final crusade won some impressive victories and sparked a 10-year truce, but the crusading spirit was fading. In 1291, Acre became the last Christian city to

Louis IX dies in Tunisia. fall. After 208 years the crusades were over.

Glossary

amok, run To behave in a confused, uncontrolled, and disruptive way

banner Flag

barricaded To block off with a barricade

besiege Surround a place with armed forces either to capture it or to force its people to surrender

bezants Gold or silver coins originally minted at Byzantium

campaign A series of military operations intended to achieve a goal, confined to a particular area, or involving a specific type of fighting

caravan A group (as of merchants or pilgrims) traveling together on a long journey through desert or dangerous regions

charismatic Of a charming, fascinating character which can inspire devotion in others

Christian A person who believes in Jesus Christ and follows his teachings

citadel A fortress, usually one on high ground above a city

dynasty A succession of rulers of the same line of descent

fanatic A person filled with excessive and single-minded zeal, especially for an extreme religious or political cause

Fatimids A political and religious dynasty that dominated an empire in the Middle East in Medieval times. Its people claimed to be descended from Fatimah, the daughter of Muhammad

Franks A member of a Germanic people living in ancient Gaul

galley A low, flat ship with one or more sails and up to three sets of oars, used for warfare and often manned by slaves or criminals

Genoese Originally from the town of Genoa in Italy

Greek fire A fire device, often launched by a flame-throwing weapon to set fire to enemy ships. It ignited on contact with water.

havoc Great confusion and disorder

Holy Land Palestine, an ancient country in southwestern Asia on the east coast of the Mediterranean Sea—a place of religious pilgrimage

Holy Roman Emperor The ruler of the Holy Roman Empire. The Holy Roman Empire existed from the 9th or 10th century to 1806 and covered most of central Europe. It was thought of as a continuation of the Western Roman Empire.

Hospitaller A member of a military religious order, originally the Knights Hospitaller were both monks and experienced soldiers

Islam A religion marked by belief in Allah as the sole deity, in Muhammad as his prophet, and in the Koran

Jesus Christ The source of the Christian religion and Savior in the Christian faith

Jerusalem Between Israel and Jordan; capital of Israel

Judaism A religion developed among the ancient Hebrews that stresses belief in one God and faithfulness to the laws of the Old Testament

looting Plunder, steal

lumbered To move heavily or clumsily

mangonel A military device used for throwing stones and other missiles

Middle Ages The period of European history from about 500 CE to about 1500

Muhammad An Arab prophet and founder of Islam

Muslim A follower of Islam

Outremer A name applied to the medieval French crusader states, including Armenia, Antioch, Tripoli, and Jerusalem.

parched Deprived of natural moisture; also: thirsty

pilgrim A person who travels to a sacred place for religious reasons

pilgrimage A journey of a pilgrim

pope The head of the Roman Catholic Church

ransom A sum of money demanded or paid for the release of a captive.

relic An object surviving from an earlier time, especially one of historical, holy, or sentimental interest

Saracens An Arab or Muslim, especially at the time of the Crusades

Seljuq The Great Seljuq Empire was a medieval Turko-Persian Empire

sepulcher A place of burial: tomb

Templar A member of the Knights Templar, who were among the most wealthy and powerful of the Western Christian military orders

trebuchet A machine used in medieval siege warfare for hurling large stones or other missiles

vizier A high official in some Muslim countries

Index